50 FINDS FROM BUCKINGHAMSHIRE

Objects from the Portable Antiquities Scheme

Arwen Wood

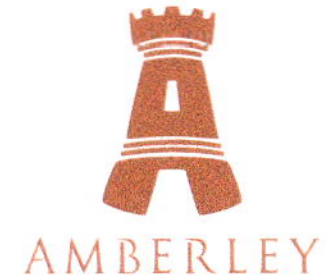

AMBERLEY

First published 2021

Amberley Publishing
The Hill, Stroud
Gloucestershire, GL5 4EP

www.amberley-books.com

ISBN 978 1 4456 9577 8 (print)
ISBN 978 1 4456 9578 5 (ebook)

British Library Cataloguing in Publication Data.
A catalogue record for this book is available from
the British Library.

Typeset in 10pt on 13pt Celeste.
Origination by Amberley Publishing.
Printed in the UK.

Contents

Acknowledgements

Firstly, and most importantly, I'd like to thank all the finders who have recorded their objects with the Portable Antiquities Scheme. By recording objects responsibly with the scheme, you have contributed personally to our knowledge and understanding of the archaeology of Buckinghamshire, and without this I could not have written this book. Also from this, research projects and a greater understanding of the county have increased, highlighting the rich diversity of the landscape and the people who have lived within it.

The finds liaison officer post in Buckinghamshire has been hosted by Bucks County Museum since 2006, providing space and storage to work at Halton Museum Stores. One of the advantages of this is I am able to work with the four keepers, and their knowledge and skills have been much appreciated and beneficial. A special thank you goes to Brett Thorn for allowing me access to the museum's collection, to photograph for this book. The museum is an important resource for archaeology in the county, and the collections both help to enlighten and provide an important resource for research of the county. By working with the museum I've also been able to carry out outreach with the community and help to inform the public on both the PAS database and archaeology in the area.

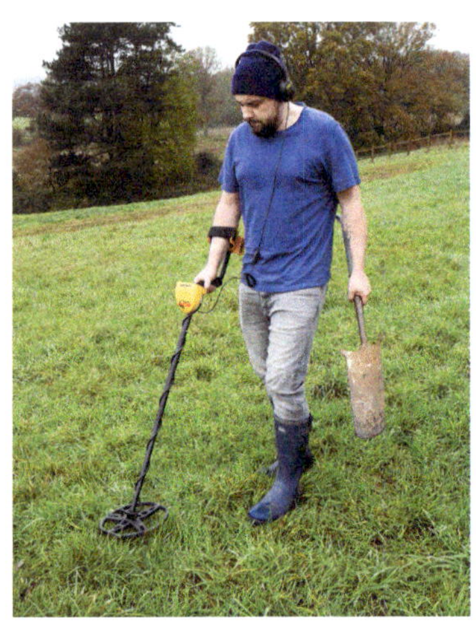

Detectorist at work. (Arwen Wood, 2019)

I have worked in the post from 2016, and I'm grateful to Ros Tyrell, my predecessor, for all the work she did, including connecting with the metal-detecting community and encouraging recording across the county.

As well as working with Bucks County Museum, I've also held finds days across the county at Old Gaol Museum in Buckingham, Milton Keynes Museum and Wycombe Museum, and I'm thankful to have been given this access. Not only has this allowed me access to finders across the county, it has also made me more aware of the heritage and enormous amount of work being carried out by local museums in this county. I appreciate it as an archaeologist and as a visitor.

A big thank you goes to the Portable Antiquities Scheme itself, and the support it is given by the British Museum. The network and knowledge of the Finds Liaison Officers, both past and present, is invaluable, and I could not do my day-to-day role without this. Some of the records and photographs in this book are the work of other FLOs, and I'm appreciative of this work. A thank you must also go to PASt Explorers, who have provided training and support to the post.

In some cases, I have not been able to use images due to copyright; for these finds more images can be found on the database records, along with more information and measurements. The majority of the photographs featured are taken from the Portable Antiquities Scheme database and while many are of my own work, some are the product of other Finds Liaison Officers. I would like to gratefully acknowledge their work here, not only for the photographs I have used but also for the specialist reports and records they have created.

Thank you to Dot Boughton, Katie Hinds, and June James for their expertise and specialist skills when writing this book; their guidance and knowledge was invaluable. Unless stated, images in this book are reproduced courtesy of the Portable Antiquities Scheme. Every attempt has been made to seek permission to reproduce photographs and images in this book, however if I have accidently used material without permission and the correct copyright I apologise and will make corrections in the future.

Finally, on a personal note, thank you to my friends and family for supporting me whilst writing this book. A special thank you goes to my husband, Edwin Wood, and our stowaway, for reading, supporting and exploring the wilds of Buckinghamshire with me.

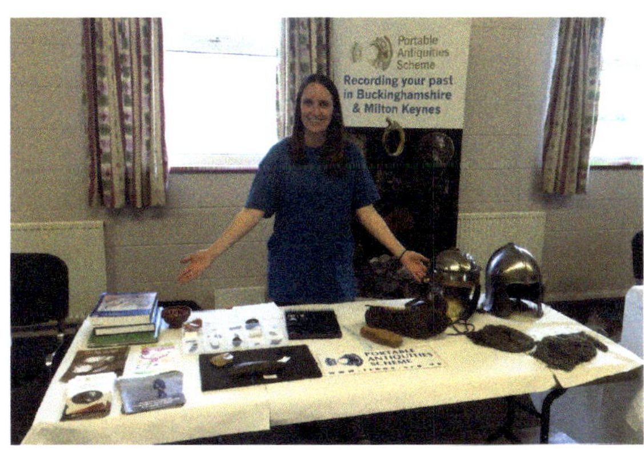

Author attending a finds day. (Edwin Wood, 2019)

Foreword by Michael Lewis

The places in which we live and work have a long past, but one that is not always obvious in the landscape around us. This is a forgotten past. Most of us know little about the people who once lived in our communities fifty years ago, let alone 500, or even 5,000 years past. Like us, they lived, played and worked here, in this place, but we know almost nothing of them.

History books tell us about royalty, great lords and important churchmen, but most others are forgotten by time. The only evidence for many of these people is the objects that they left behind; sometimes buried on purpose, but more often lost by chance. Occasionally, through archaeological fieldwork, we can place these objects in a context that allows us to better understand the past, but nowadays excavation is mostly development-led, so only takes place when a new building, road or service pipe, is being constructed.

A unique way of understanding the past is through the finds recorded through the Portable Antiquities Scheme, and those chosen here by Arwen Wood (Finds Liaison Officer for Buckinghamshire) are just fifty of over 5,000 from Buckinghamshire on its database (www.finds.org.uk). These finds are all discovered by the public, most by metal-detector users, searching in places archaeologists are unlikely to go or otherwise excavate. As such they provide important clues of underlying archaeology that, once recorded, help archaeologists understand our past – a past of the people, found by the people.

Some of these finds are truly magnificent, others less imposing. Yet, like pieces in a jigsaw puzzle they are often meaningless alone, but once placed together paint a picture. These finds therefore allow us to understand the story of people who once lived here, in Buckinghamshire.

Dr Michael Lewis
Head of Portable Antiquities & Treasure
British Museum

Introduction

The Portable Antiquities Scheme (PAS) is a national scheme funded by the British Museum and hosted by institutions across England and Wales. To date forty Finds Liaison Officers (FLOs) are employed across the country to work with members of the public to record archaeological objects and provide outreach and support.

The finds I have selected are a personal choice based on my three and a half years in the post. Buckinghamshire and Milton Keynes were new areas to me when I moved here from Hampshire in May 2016 and exploring and learning about this new county has been stimulating and helped motivate me in the recording of the finds. When looking through the database there were other finds that could have been included; the ones here are a representative of the many more recorded and hopefully help to bring the landscape alive.

The post has been based at Buckinghamshire County Museum since 2003. The museum is located in Aylesbury, in the centre of the county. The museum is housed in one of the remaining historic buildings in the old town and has building features from different periods including Tudor wall paintings. The Museum Resource Centre is the main repository for excavated archaeological material. The museum tells the history of the county, from geological formation to the present, highlighting the communities that have lived here. A number of artefacts depicted in this book are part of this collection. The museum actively collects archaeology, including treasure, as a way of enriching our knowledge.

Buckinghamshire is a long county bordering Oxfordshire, Northamptonshire, Bedfordshire, Hertfordshire and Berkshire. The lower part of the county sits in the Thames Valley, with the Chiltern Hills crossing the centre, and to the north the unitary authority of Milton Keynes. This has created a diverse county with distinct identities existing in the north, centre and south. The chalk of the Chilterns, once the bed of a warm shallow sea that existed during the cretaceous at the very end of the reign of the dinosaurs, provided the flint for the early inhabitants of the area, as will be seen in following chapters. The fertile post-glacial soils helped support farming from the Neolithic to the present. While the high points that once provided places to watch and guard the region are now in many places part of an Area of Outstanding Natural Beauty, which can be enjoyed by all.

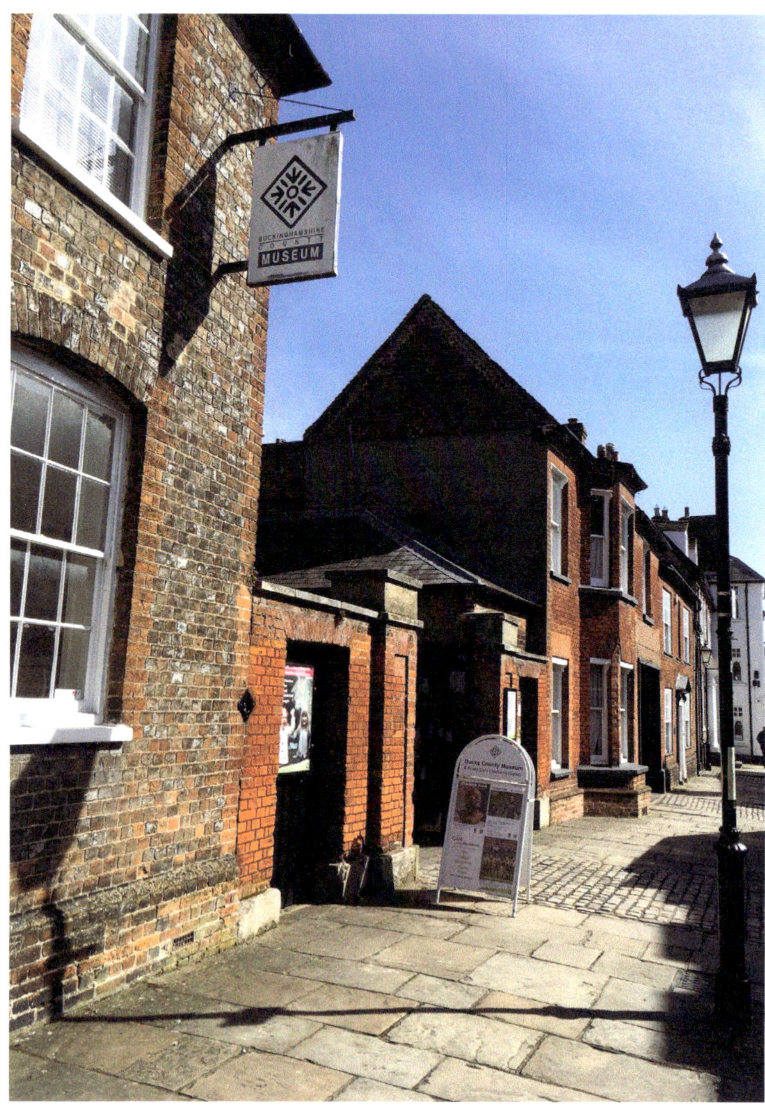

Bucks County Museum, in Aylesbury. (Arwen Wood, 2019)

As part of the recording process it is important to have accurate findspots. By having these findspots it has allowed archaeologists to study the landscape and discover new sites. Research projects also use this data to uncover more about the history of our county's landscape. By using this findspot data it has allowed me to generate the maps used in this book.

When I first moved to Buckinghamshire, I was informed that I was taking on a county that had no standing archaeology and was simply a county that people in history used to pass through. It is my ambition to, in part, dispel this misconception and convey the vibrant and interesting archaeology that is to be found within the borders. It should be remembered when reading this book that archaeology is about people, and the objects contained within are interesting only in so far as what they can tell us about them. Each object can tell us about their everyday lives, the shifting currents of fashion, identity, and perhaps even their hopes and dreams.

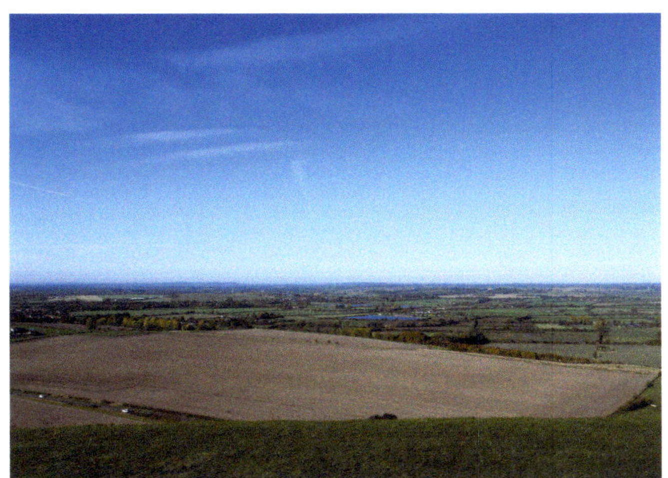

View of Buckinghamshire
taken from Ivinghoe Beacon.
(Arwen Wood, 2019)

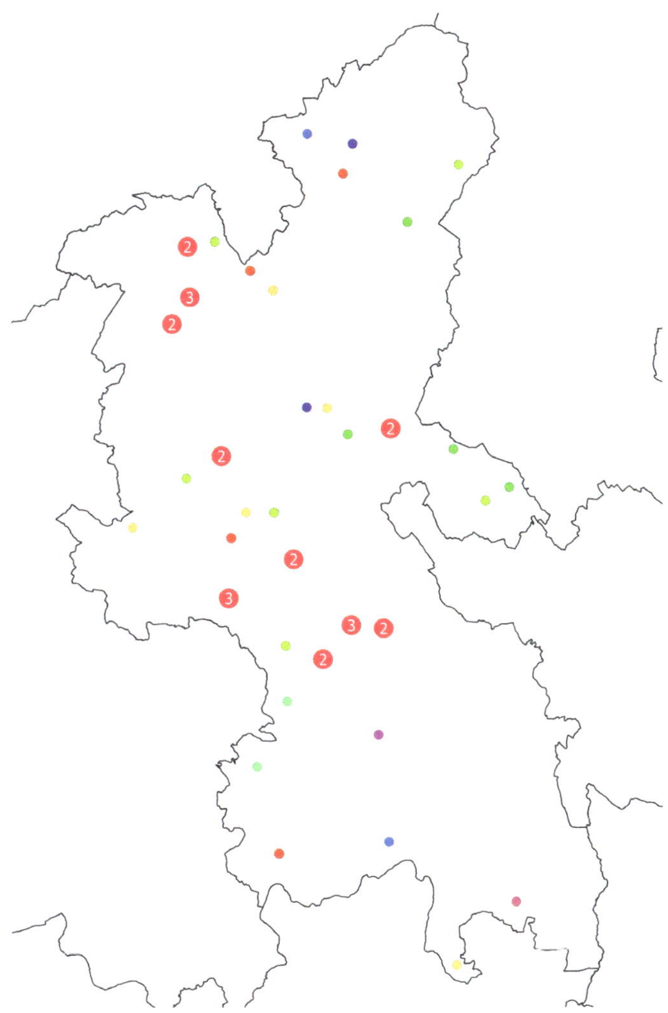

Map of Buckinghamshire,
showing the fifty finds.
(Edwin Wood, 2019)

Chapter 1
Prehistoric Buckinghamshire

Early humans first appeared in Britain in the Lower Palaeolithic, around 700,000 years ago. These early humans were different species to modern humans and included *Homo neanderthalensis* and *Homo heidelbergensis.* Most of the evidence for this is found in areas such as the Norfolk coast, where sites such as Happisburgh provide tantalising glimpses of the distant past. Evidence for the hunting activities and tool making of species such as *Homo heidelbergensis* has been found at Boxgrove in Sussex dating to 500,000 years ago.

The glaciation or Ice Age began in Britain around 480,000 years ago, and had a great effect on the earliest humans, pushing them back across to what is now mainland Europe. Successive waves of glaciation and retreat would expose then cover areas of the country over thousands of years. In Buckinghamshire the evidence for this period is sparse, with no early human skeletal remains being found in the county, so we therefore rely on the individual finds to piece together this early period in human history. The Upper Palaeolithic or Late Stone Age began around 40,000 years ago, and it is around this time that modern humans begin to appear in Europe co-existing and eventually supplanting the local Neanderthal populations. Few sites have been found dating to this period; however, in Buckinghamshire the important site of Pitstone was found to have bones from mammoth, lion, wolf and bears.

This period is defined by the stone tools that the early humans made and used. These tools were predominantly of flint, though other stones, such as basalt, chert and greenstone were also utilised depending on local availability. Most organic materials do not survive archaeologically except under exceptional circumstances, such as waterlogging, extreme aridity or frozen in permafrost. It is the changes in the technology and manufacture of stone tools that allow archaeologists to date them to different periods and understand how they developed over time. The introduction of soft hammer techniques, pressure flaking, and other technologies allowed different tool types and cultures to develop.

It can be difficult to identify worked flint and stone tools, but features such as striking platforms, retouch and fractures can help to recognise the different types of tools. A flint tool is created by striking a stone core with a soft or hard hammer at an angle, forcing the flint to flake off. This creates ripples in the surface of the flint called conchoidal fracture, and further working around the edges of the flake to create a durable working edge is

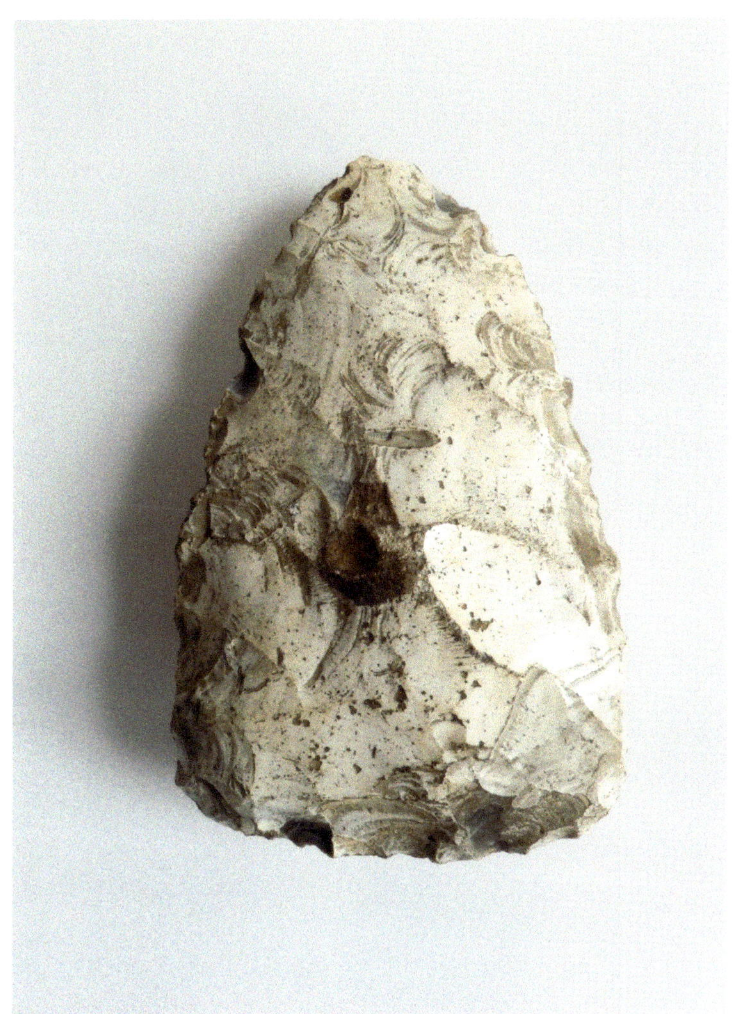

Palaeolithic handaxe found in Bourne End, and thought to be made by Neanderthal. (Arwen Wood/ BCM, 2019)

called retouch. In Buckinghamshire, flints found in the Chilterns often have a white chalk colour to the surface, whereas flints from other areas of Buckinghamshire can be a more orange-brown colour. This colouration is due to the geology from which the flint originates and the reaction of the outer surface with the soil or surrounding rock.

The Palaeolithic Period

This period is characterised by objects such as handaxes, scrapers, and Levallois technology. In Buckinghamshire, these objects are typically found on the river terraces and where deep gravel extraction has taken place. However, through the Historic Environment Record and the Portable Antiquities Scheme, the occasional chance find has been recorded, adding to the tantalising evidence of this enigmatic period across Buckinghamshire.

This Palaeolithic handaxe was found in the south of the county. The flint has been knapped on both sides, something known as bifacial working, and would have created a sharp edge for the user to utilise. It is thought that handaxes such as this would have been used for cutting organic materials, such as meat or plant material. They were essential tools for survival in the harsh world of the Palaeolithic, used for hunting and for gathering the resources early humans needed. This example has been tentatively dated as 50,000 to 15,000 BC; such a broad date range is due to the lack of additional archaeological evidence found with the handaxe. As with all finds, without having the object in context it is difficult to narrow it down to a more precise date.

The picture of the Palaeolithic period in Buckinghamshire is far from complete, and knowledge will continue to grow as archaeology and finds are recorded and researched further.

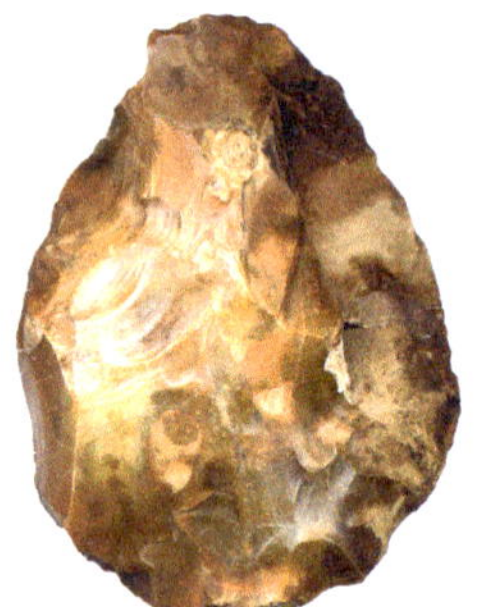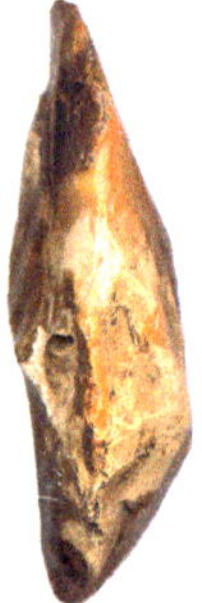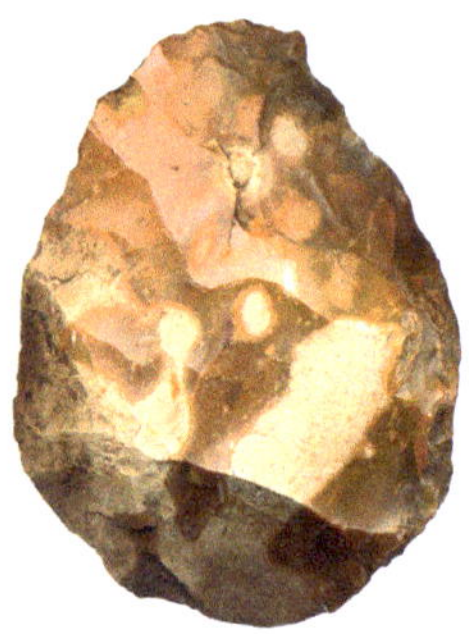

BUC-C48B16 Palaeolithic handaxe. (Arwen Wood/BCM, 2019)

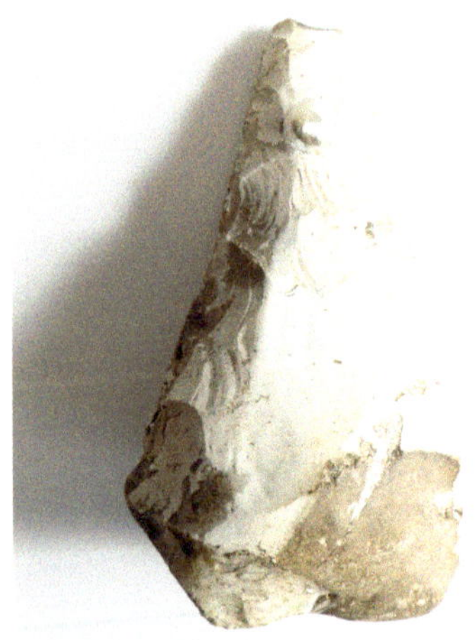

Flint handaxe found in Seer Green, AYBCM L169. (Arwen Wood/BCM, 2019)

The Palaeolithic period finishes at the end of the Ice Age about 10,000 years ago and is followed by the Mesolithic or Middle Stone Age. With the ice sheets receding across Britain the movement of animals and early humans became easier, though the landscape and climate were changing. It is during this period that Britain becomes an island, as the area known as Doggerland is slowly flooded by rising sea levels in the North Sea. Archaeological evidence for the submerged landscape, its wildlife and the human occupants is frequently found during dredging and deep-sea trawler fishing. In Buckinghamshire, as with the Palaeolithic, most of the evidence is found near the rivers, and in the occasional chance find.

The people that lived in Britain in the Mesolithic are thought to be nomadic hunter-gatherers adapting to the change of climate. A wide variety of animals became extinct in Britain and across north-west Europe, as they were unable to cope with the loss of habitat and changing climate caused by the retreat of the glaciers. Typical finds from this period include flint cores, used to create small flakes or microliths for use as arrowheads, and tranchet axes, a type of axe probably used for working wood. The presence of flint scatters and concentrations of flint-working debris can indicate seasonal campsites or areas used for hunting. An example of a flint core can be seen below with some associated bladelets and microliths. The core would have been hit by a hard hammer such as a stone, or a soft hammer such as an antler, at the top to create small flint blades that could be worked and retouched to make microliths.

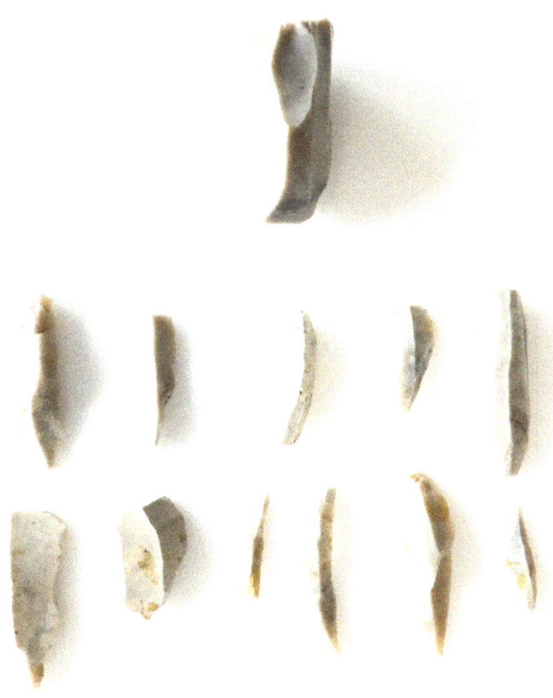

Core and microliths dating from the Early Mesolithic period, AYBCM 8.64. (Arwen Wood/ BCM, 2019)

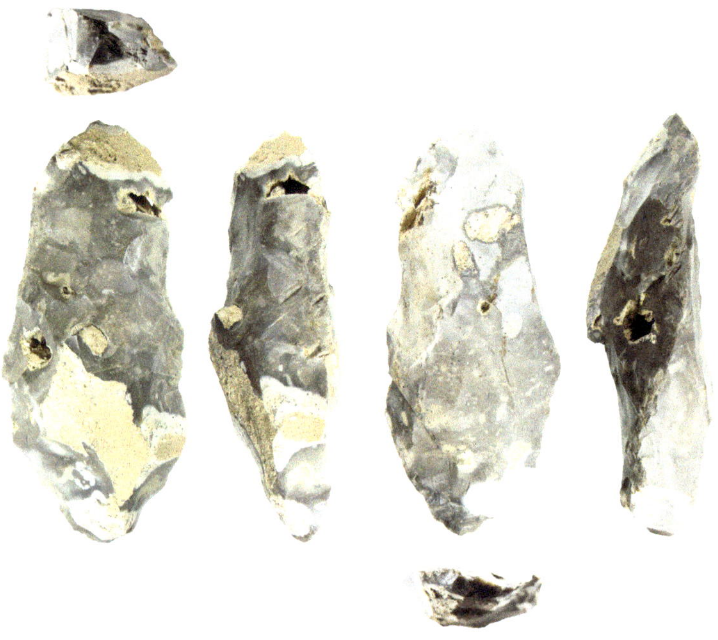

BUC-C99C18,
a Mesolithic
tranchet axehead.

This tranchet axehead or adze dates to the Early Mesolithic, *c.* 9000–8000 BC. Made of a patchy, light-grey flint it still retains some of the original outer cortex. In this example the cortex is white from the chalk in which the flint formed. Like the earlier handaxe, this axehead has been bifacially flaked giving the object a characteristic triangular cross-section. Often known as a 'Thames Pick', because of their distribution in the Thames Valley, these axes are often less symmetrical and retain substantial amounts of cortex on the surface. The flint is of poor quality, containing numerous natural voids within the structure of the flint. These voids are caused by either flaws in the material during formation, or sometimes by trace fossils of burrowing marine invertebrates.

Neolithic

The Mesolithic period transitions into the Neolithic or New Stone Age at *c.* 4500 to 4000 BC. The Neolithic is categorised by people starting to make their mark on the landscape, with small permanent settlements. This revolution was triggered by the domestication of crops and animals, a technology originating in the Middle East. It meant that people were no longer reliant on following the herds to hunt and the seasonal plants but instead were able to produce food through agriculture. As the population became more settled, it made more of a lasting mark on the landscape. This in turn means that there is more evidence to be found by archaeologists, such as causewayed enclosures, settlement sites and long barrows. Whiteleaf Barrow stands on a prominent hill close to Princes Risborough and the burial found within it is believed to date to *c.* 3700 BC. A causewayed enclosure is a concentrically ditched enclosure with a causeway traversing the ditches. In the south of the county, causewayed enclosures have been found at Dorney and Eton, and in the north a cursus dating from the Early Neolithic has been found near Wolverton. A cursus is a long, parallel-ditched enclosure varying in length from 50 yards to 60 miles. Their function is unknown but is thought to have been related to ceremonial activity. Perhaps the most well-known example is the cursus in the Stonehenge landscape, which is approximately 3 kilometres (1.9 miles) in length.

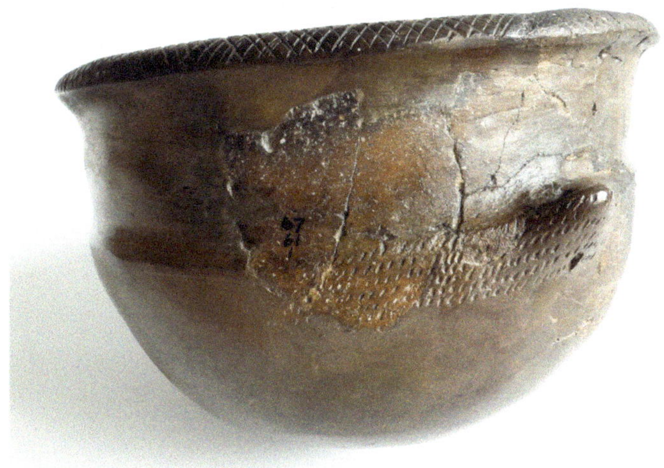

Whiteleaf bowl.
(Arwen Wood/
BCM, 2019)

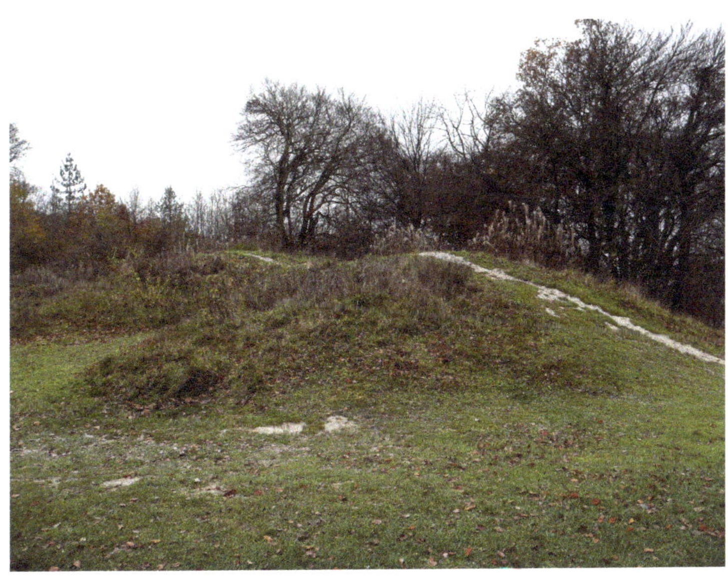

Whiteleaf Barrow.
(Arwen Wood, 2019)

As the name suggests, this period remains dominated by stone technology including polished stone axes and barbed and tanged arrowheads. However, perhaps most excitingly for the archaeologist, the Neolithic sees the first use of pottery. Ceramics are the principal method archaeologists use to date sites as the decoration and forms of vessels change relatively rapidly over time. Research has also been done to examine where the raw materials were sourced and so demonstrate potential links of exchange or centres of production. Pottery would have been decorated by imprinting fingers, or everyday objects such as cordage, wood, or flint. An example of this decoration can be seen on the Mortlake ware bowl (see below).

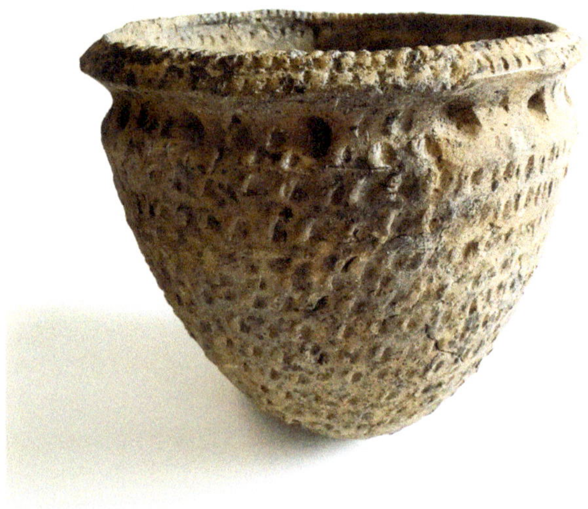

Mid to Late Neolithic Mortlake bowl, AYBCM 2010 141.1195. (Arwen Wood/ BCM, 2019)

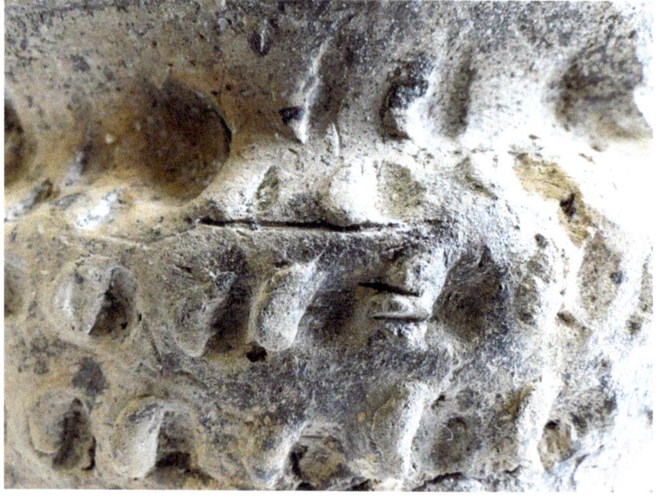

Close up of the Mortlake bowl, showing decoration detail. (Arwen Wood/ BCM, 2019)

This is a Neolithic polished and ground axehead, dating to *c.* 3500–2100 BC. The axehead is made of flint and has been ground smooth to produce a polished surface with a curved cutting edge. This type of axehead would have been set into a wooden haft and cord or twine would have then been wrapped around the haft and the axehead to hold it in place. The colours of this axehead are slightly unusual as this artefact was found by divers, submerged. The flint roughout would have been ground onto another piece of stone, such as granite or sandstone, to produce the smooth surface, a process that would have taken many hours of intense labour.

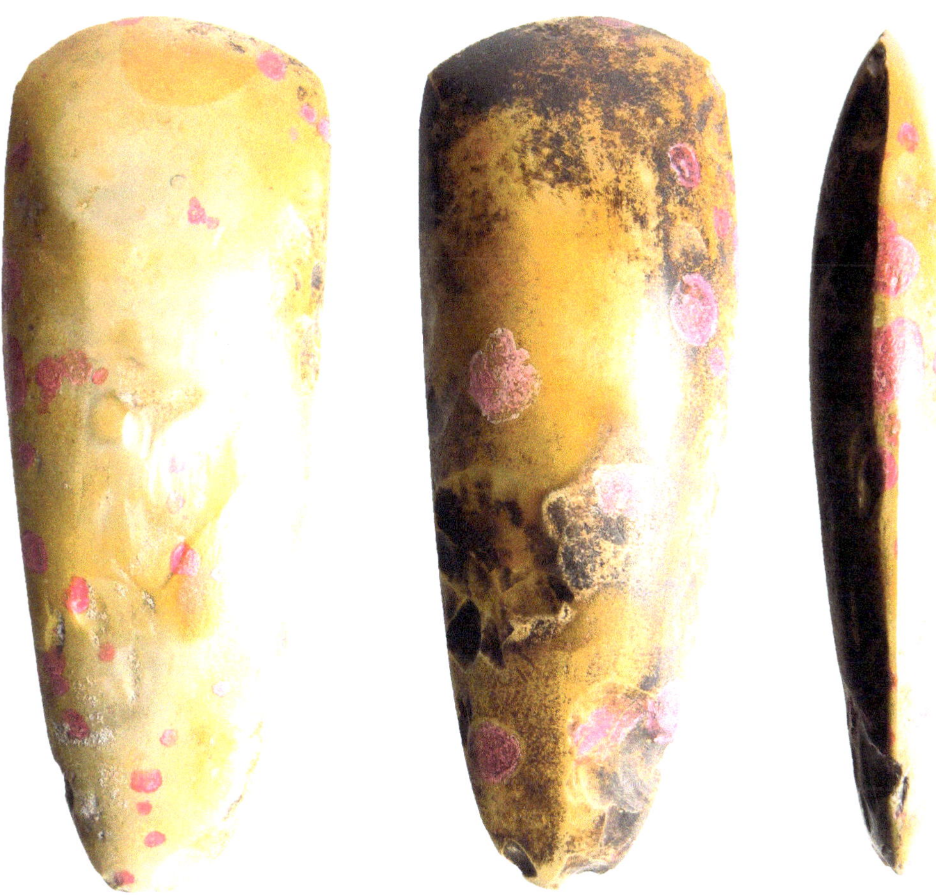

BERK-945612, a Neolithic axehead.

A much smaller flint tool is the distinctly shaped barbed and tanged arrowhead, so named for the rear-facing barbs on each side of the head and the tang used to attach it to the shaft. These arrowheads date from the Late Neolithic to the Early Bronze Age, at *c.* 2500–1150 BC, and are typical of this transitional period. The flint itself is shaped from a larger piece using a stone, then using a technique called pressure flaking small flakes are removed during retouch to delicately create the barbs and tang. To do this a soft hammer or point would have been used – typically these were made from antler. Both sides of the flint are retouched to create the razor-sharp edge and the barbs would have caused the arrow to dig into the target on impact, causing more damage to the subject with every movement. This arrowhead was found near Milton Keynes in a ploughed field.

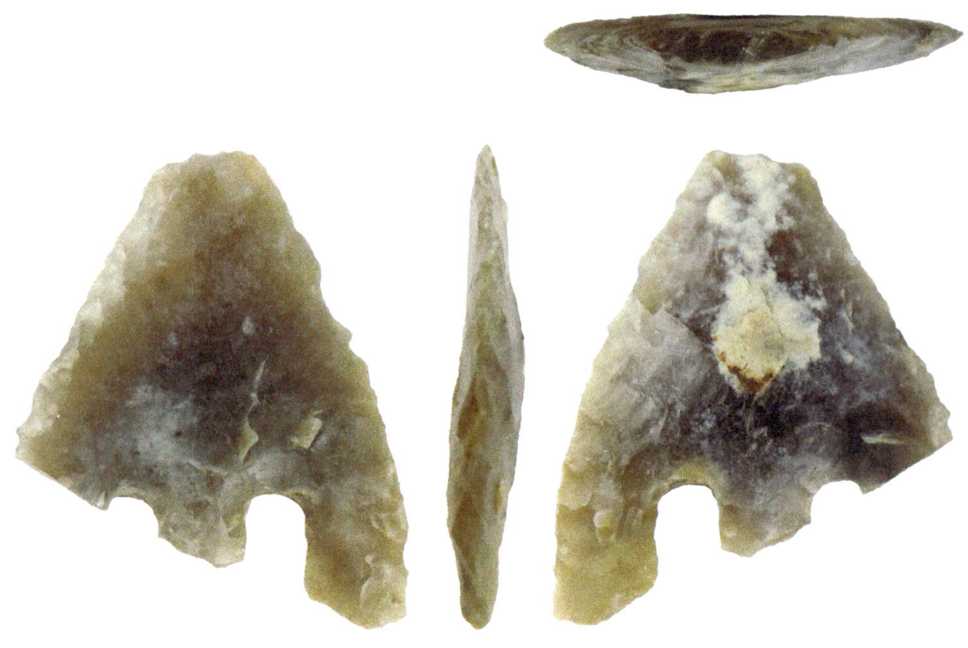

A Late Neolithic to Early Bronze Age barbed and tanged arrowhead, BUC-D791B2.

Chapter 2
The Bronze Age in Buckinghamshire

The Bronze Age in Britain dates from the period 2350–800 BC and marks the beginnings of the production of metalworking in Britain, including the use of copper alloy, gold and silver. As the raw materials for these metals are not found in Buckinghamshire, either the resources or the objects themselves would have been brought in, suggesting a trade or barter system existed. Flint was still used extensively during the period as metal objects remained relatively rare. As metalworking becomes more widespread, communities were no longer limited by the materials of flint and stone tools, and a wider range of objects are found from this period, including tools and jewellery. As metals tend to survive well over a long period, more evidence is available to archaeologists, and the durability of decorative schemes and styles allows us to postulate ideas about different cultural groups.

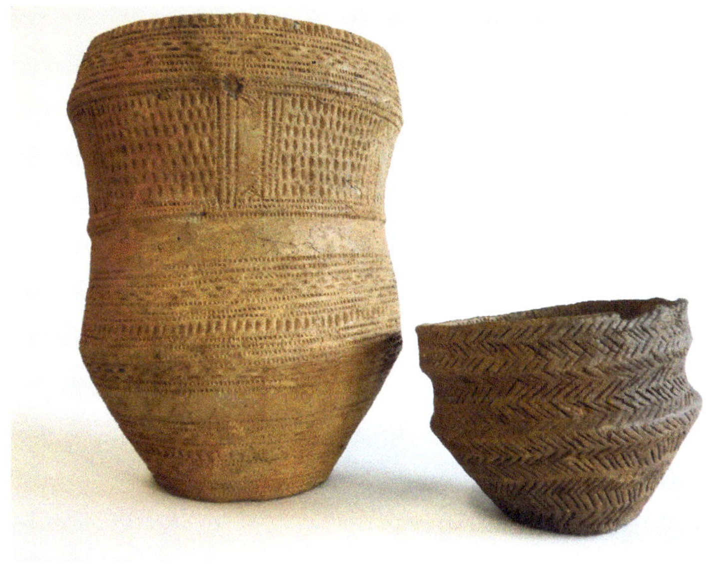

Beaker pot (l301) and a small food vessel found in Buckinghamshire, AYBCM 1954.3. (Arwen Wood/ BCM, 2019)

Other materials should not be forgotten, however, and it is during the Bronze Age that the Beaker culture spreads across Europe. This is characterised by a distinctive burial custom, which included the placing of 'Beaker' decorated pottery into graves. Beaker burials have been found in Buckinghamshire, including sites in Bierton, Ravenstone and Chesham.

Evidence is also visible in the landscape, and features such as round barrows are typical of the earlier part of the period. These features remained prominent throughout history and some attracted use in later periods or inspired folklore, some of which endures to this day. While some barrows would have contained Beaker burial inhumations, the majority have been found to be cremations. Other Bronze Age features in the landscape include settlement evidence such as ring ditches, settlement sites categorised by post holes and pits, and Late Bronze Age hill fort enclosures such as Ivinghoe Beacon.

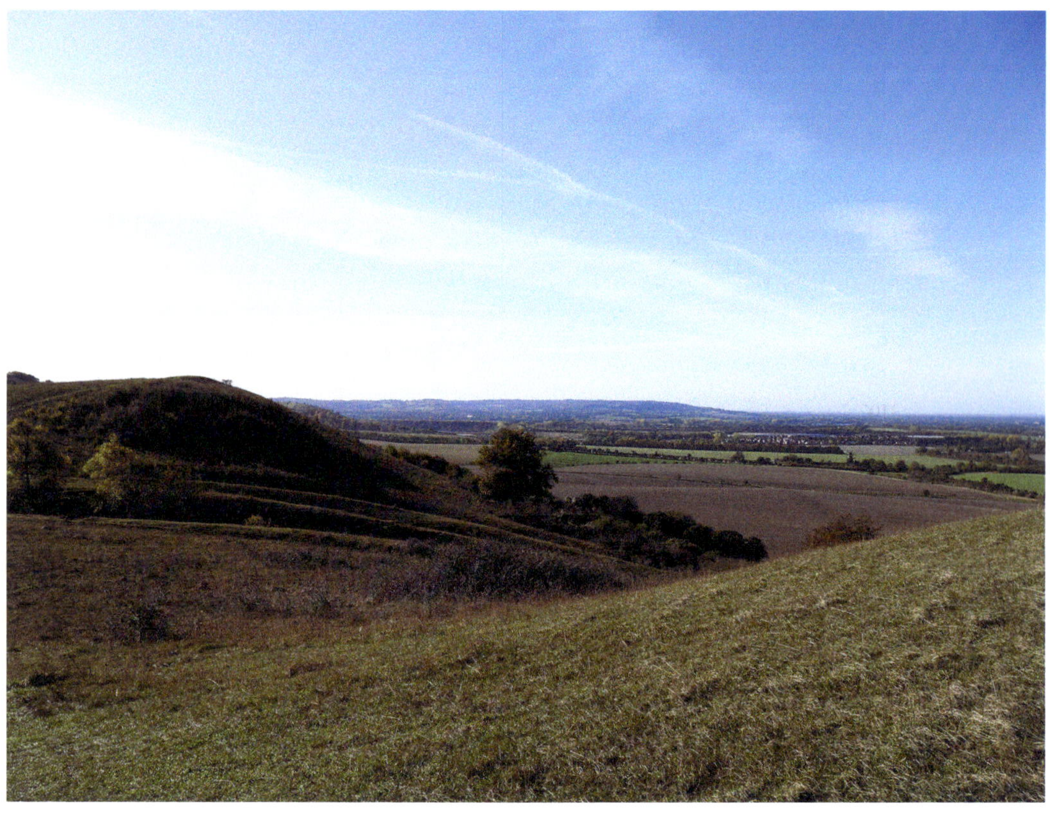

The earthworks at Ivinghoe Beacon. (Arwen Wood, 2019)

This mysterious object is often erroneously called 'ring money', though there is no evidence for their use as currency and they are thought to be more ornamental in their use. It is made with stripes of yellow and paler gold, the paler type has tarnished and is now a black colour. When it was analysed by specialists it was found to be solid. This is significant as some penannular rings are found to have a base metal core, with the gold covering. This example was found to have a gold content of around 78 per cent, and also contained silver. Different theories surround these objects but is possible that it was a type of jewellery, such as a hair ornament or a nose ring. Objects such as these date to the Late Bronze Age.

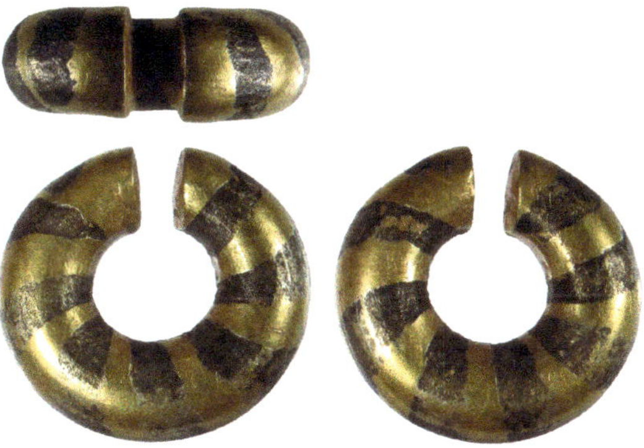

BUC-A73107, a gold penannular ring.

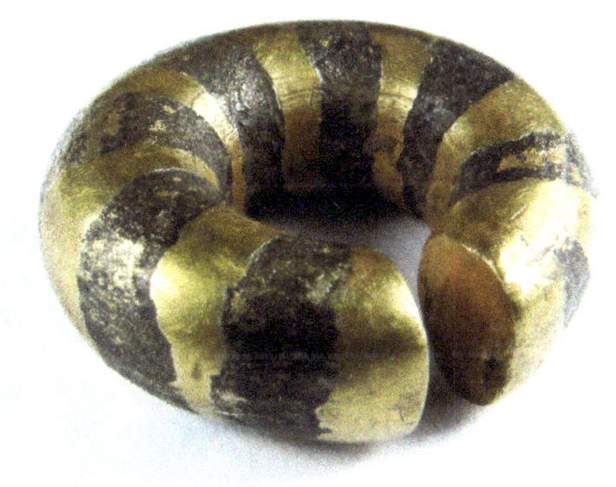

BUC-A73107, a gold penannular ring.

This socketed spearhead dates from around 1500 to 1300 BC, placing it in the Middle Bronze Age. It has a pronounced midrib, with loops half-way down the socket of the spearhead. It was thought that the loops would have been used to attach or hold the spearhead onto the shaft using cordage or leather. The shaft would have sat in the socket of the spearhead. Like all copper alloy objects from this period the spearhead would have been cast in a mould, these were made from a range of materials such as clay, sand, stone and bronze. Weapons like this were most likely used for hunting though they would also have served martial functions. Complete examples are unusual and often only fragments are found, some of which display the signs of having been ritually broken or 'killed'.

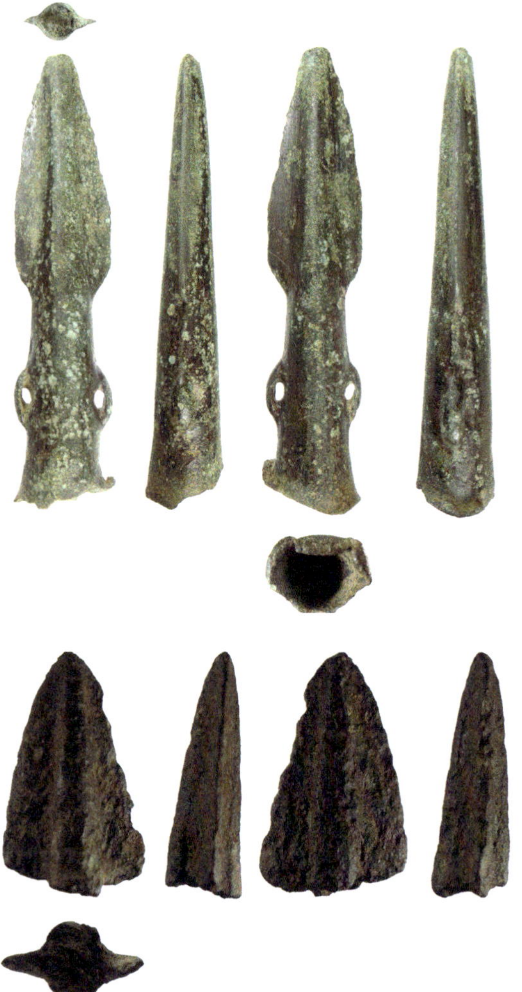

BUC-884358, a Middle Bronze Age socketed spearhead.

BUC-D45507, a fragment of the tip of a spearhead found in Mentmore.

This scabbard chape was found on the borders of Bedfordshire and Buckinghamshire, close to the River Ouzel and dates to the Late Bronze Age, 1150–800 BC. This is an unusual find for Buckinghamshire and has been designated of regional importance. It is a functional object and would have been attached to the end of a leather scabbard, in which a sword would have been held. This would have prevented the blade cutting through the bottom of the sheath and protected the owner of the blade, and also protected the point of the sword from damage. Besides this practical function, the chape served to embellish the scabbard and draw attention to the weapon, displaying the status of the owner. The decorative quality of chapes is demonstrated by the range of types and numbers that have been found from this period, with another example being this bag-shaped chape found in Dorset. Tongue-shaped chapes, similar to the example illustrated here, were found as part of the Guilsfield Hoard, which has also been dated to the Late Bronze Age.

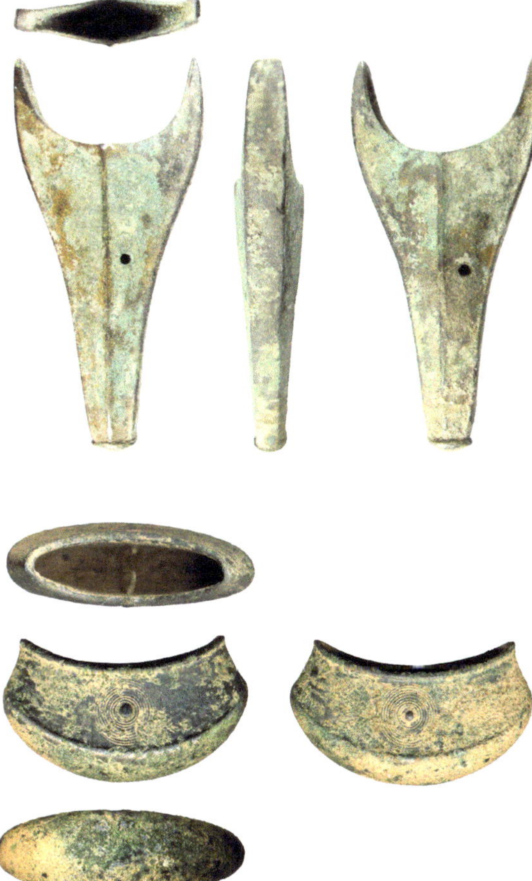

BUC-E3E35D, a Late Bronze Age
scabbard chape.

DOR-BD9AED, a bag-shaped chape,
found in Dorset.

8. BUC-C07E88 Gold Torc
Found in 2009 in Ellesborough

These two gold ribbon torcs date from the Middle Bronze Age, 1400–1150 BC. A torc was an item of jewellery worn around the neck, and was made of coiled, twisted, or strips of metal. Rather mysteriously one of the torcs has been folded in eight places, and the other has been rolled up, possibly as a way of ritually removing them from use. At the ends of the torcs the ribbon narrows and folds over on itself to create a hook. This would have been used as a fastener to clasp the ends of the object together and to hold it in place securely. These torcs are similar to ones found in Somerset dating to this period, and it is thought that they could also have been worn as bracelets due to the way the ribbon has been doubled over. Another interpretation is that the hook fastener could have attached to the folded ribbon.

Gold was highly valued in the Bronze Age, and objects such as these demonstrate that craftsmen of the period were very highly skilled. Gold was mostly used for making jewellery and clothing fittings as it is too soft for use as a tool. The people who wore such items were quite literally wearing their wealth, displaying their status using a vibrant and rare material.

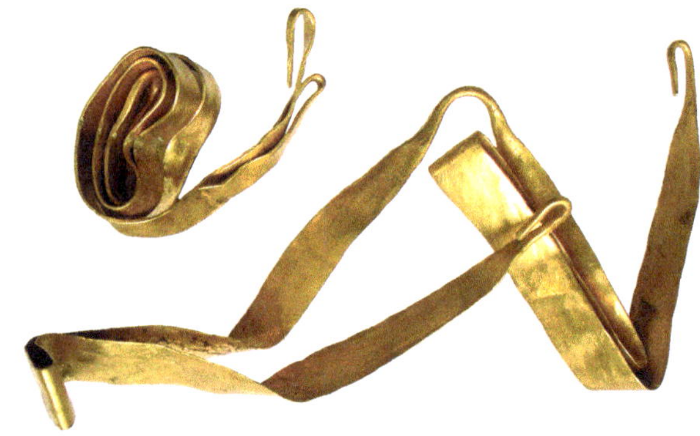

BUC-C07E88, a gold torc.

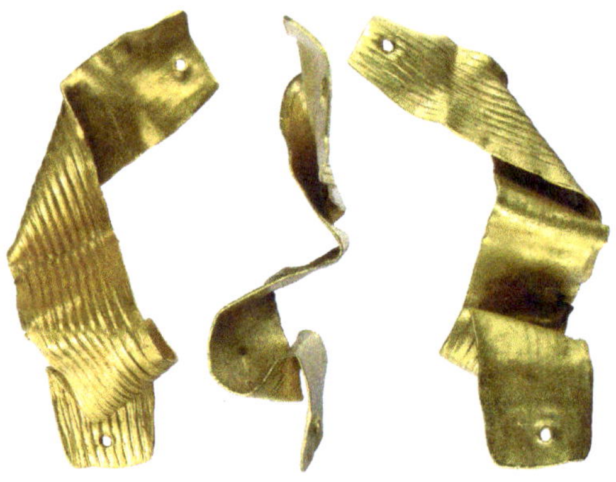

BUC-26AB57, a gold strip found in Milton Keynes.

This is the blade of a Middle to Late Bronze Age dagger, dating to 1300–1150 BC. The blade would have originally had a wooden handle attached, and there are projections which would have held this in place. Sword and dagger hilts were commonly made of organic material such as bone or wood, so do not usually survive, except in extremely rare circumstances. As a lot of metal was used to create a sword such as this, it would have belonged to someone of high status. Swords are often said to be the only weapons designed specifically for use against other people and demonstrate a strong warrior culture. Their use as ritual offerings again shows their value, as offering such an expensive item to the gods would have elevated the status of the giver.

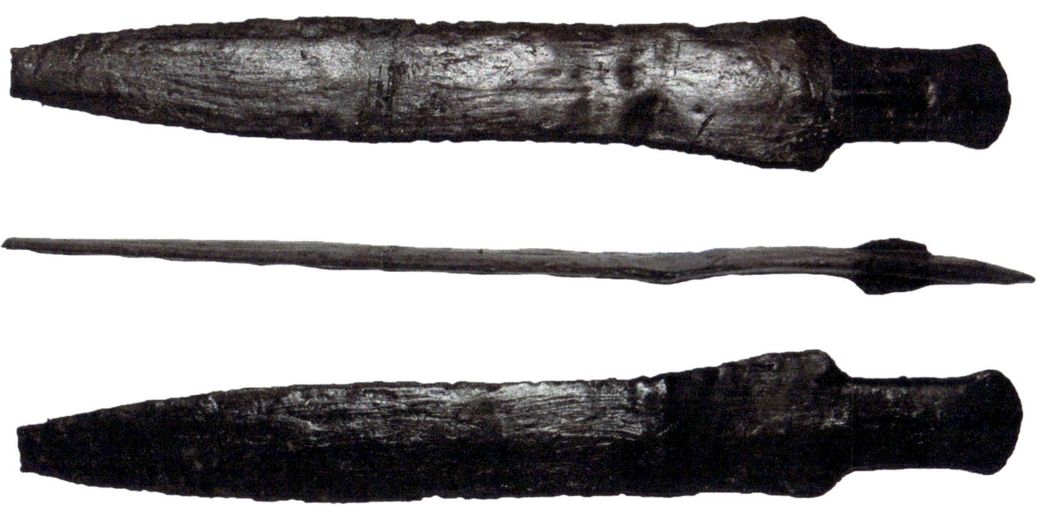

BH-2DF409, a dagger.

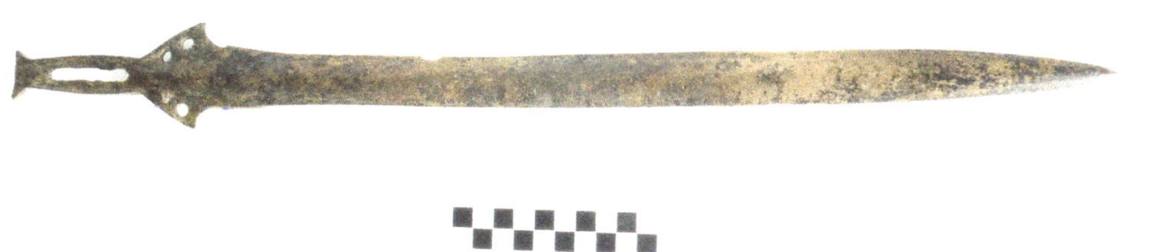

Bronze sword found in a river deposit in Newport Pagnall, AYBCM 1999.12.1. (Arwen Wood/ BCM, 2019)

Objects made of bronze in this period tend to be made of an alloy of around 90 per cent copper, with the other 10 per cent a mixture of other metals, including tin or lead. Copper in Britain is found in Wales, Scotland, Ireland, Cornwall and Devon. To start with, the copper ore would have been collected in rocks, crushed and then separated by hand. Separation by water may have also been used. The copper ore would then have been smelted, with heat reaching 1000 degrees to achieve this. The liquid metal would then be poured into a mould. While these are not often found, one was recorded by the PAS in 2017, from a site in Oxfordshire. This mould was for a Middle Bronze Age palstave axe, similar to the one below, and consisted of two halves or valves. As these were two objects found together of prehistoric date, and made of metal, they qualify as potential treasure under the Treasure Act 1996 and are recorded as treasure number 2017T202.

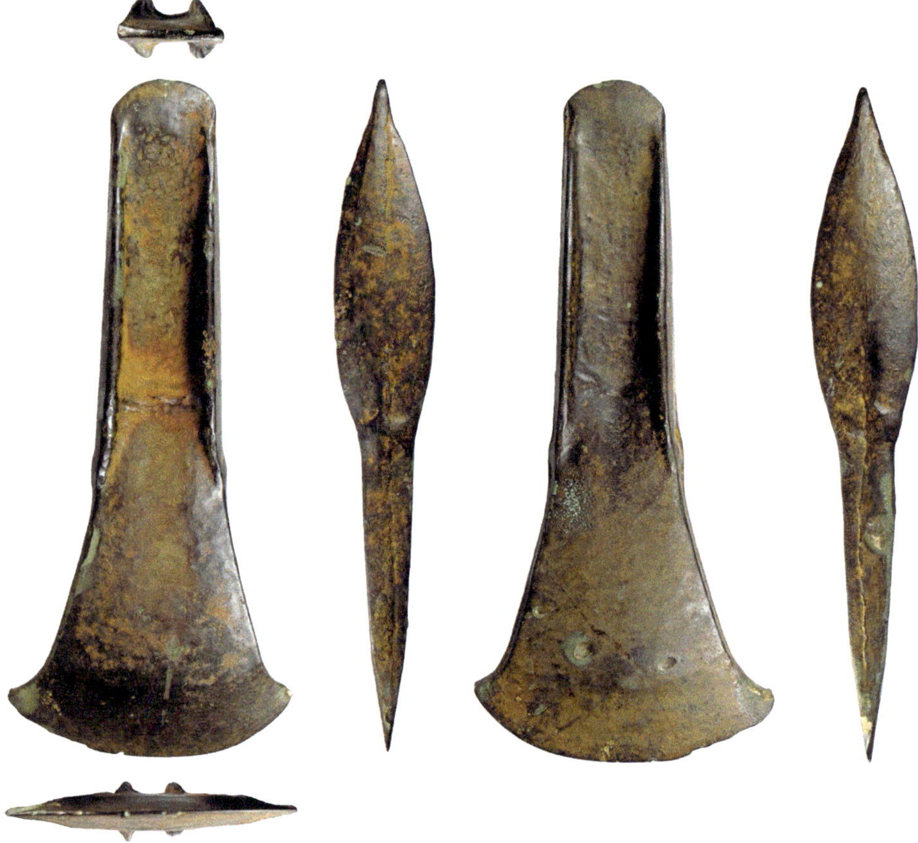

BUC-722493, palstave axehead.

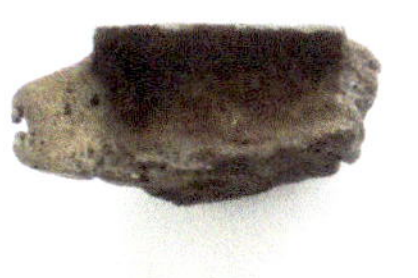

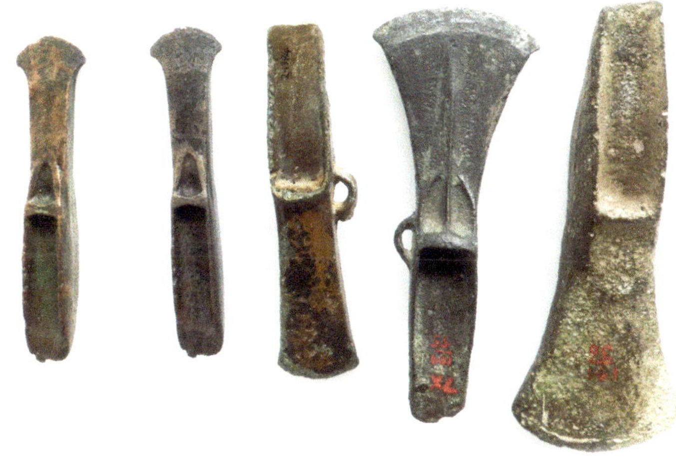

Different types of palstave axeheads from the museum collection. (Arwen Wood/BCM, 2019)

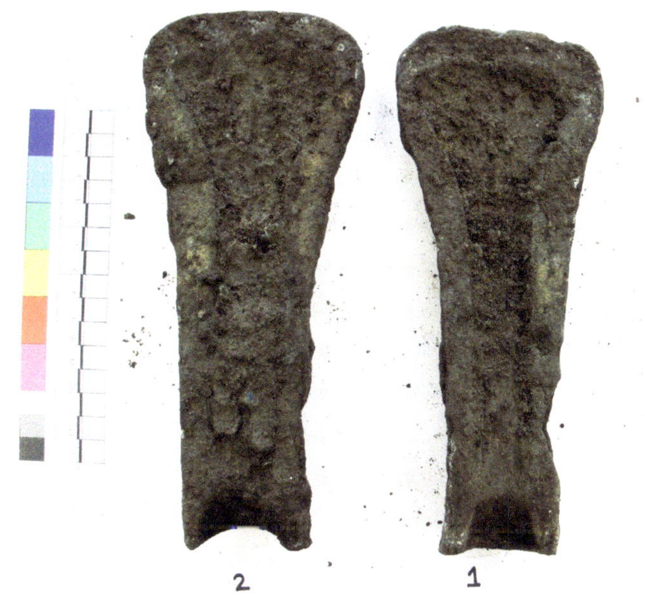

BUC-7E5EA8 Middle Bronze Age palstave mould, found in Oxfordshire before cleaning. (Arwen Wood/BCM, 2017)

Sometimes the function of an object is not always apparent. This object is thought to date from the Middle Bronze Age to the Middle Iron Age, 1500–300 BC. To date, about forty-eight of these objects have been recorded by the PAS and are known as 'moustache-shaped' due to their distinct form. A similar object was found in the Salisbury Hoard, allowing archaeologists to date these objects to this period. The narrow cross-section in this object suggests that it was used as an attachment, or that something was fitted to it. The object bares similarities to wing-shaped scabbard chapes, however the object seems small in comparison and it is unlikely it was used for this. Objects such as this are important to record even if it is unsure of the use, as new ideas and knowledge are always being developed, and it is possible that a new discovery in the future will reveal what these objects were for.

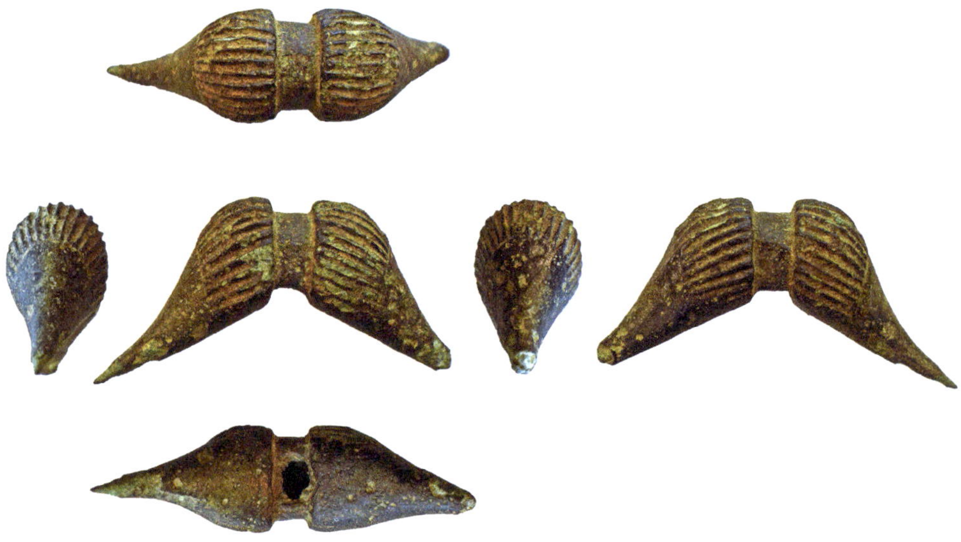

NARC-6A4546 unidentified object.

Hoards of metal artefacts are also found in this period and can be composed of multiple bronze axeheads or palstaves, or gold jewellery as with this assemblage found in Milton Keynes. The hoard was found in the remains of a pottery vessel, and comprised of two gold neck rings, three gold bracelets and a small fragment of copper alloy wire. This was an unusual find as hoards from the Middle to Late Bronze Age rarely contain both gold and pottery objects. The Milton Keynes hoard is on display at the British Museum.

Chapter 3
The Iron Age

The Iron Age in Buckinghamshire dates from around 800 BC, and traditionally ends with the arrival of the Romans in AD 43, however local customs and culture continued after this date. It is important to remember that the partitioning of time into separate periods is a modern imposition on the past and, for most of the people of Britain, life would have continued as before. This period gets its name from the development and use of iron, which occurred during it and which gradually replaced copper alloys as the material used to produce weapons and tools. Iron objects are less well represented on the Portable Antiquities Scheme database, and indeed in wider archaeology, due to the poor preservation of the material, and can often only be identified by x-raying the object to see through the layers of corrosion.

In the Early Iron Age, settlements and features from the Bronze Age such as field systems continue to be used, and some of the hill forts that are found in Buckinghamshire originate from the earlier period. This includes Ivinghoe Beacon and Boddington Hill Fort, which have been found to be of Late Bronze Age date. The continued use of earlier settlements demonstrates the continuity of communities within the area, and their connection to the landscape. There are more than seventeen hill forts in Buckinghamshire, most of which are to be found following the line of the Chiltern Hills, a natural barrier between the Thames Basin to the south and wider plains to the north.

Iron Age settlements have been found across the county, and one of the main features of these settlements are the roundhouses. At Walton, a settlement consisting of five roundhouses has been investigated, and a large roundhouse with possible feasting links has been found at Bancroft.

The Late Iron Age also sees the introduction and circulation of coinage into Britain, starting with Gallo-Belgic gold coins thought to have come in with trade. British coins were influenced by the coins made on the Continent and were often stylised copies of Greek or Macedonian coins. Later coins also copied the style of Roman issues, perhaps as a way of expressing allegiance or power by association. The coins are thought to be issued by the different British tribes, and distributions of the coins can help to demonstrate the influence of tribal leaders. Coins found north of the Thames and the Chilterns area are usually of the Catuvellauni tribe, a group centred on Verulamium, modern St Albans. This tribe came to dominate their neighbours including the Trinovantes of Essex, with whom they seem to have formed a union in the decades immediately prior to the Roman conquest. One of the most well-known rulers in the Iron Age was Cunobelin of the Catuvellauni, who was recognised by the Romans as a powerful ruler and was immortalised in the Shakespeare play *Cymbeline.*

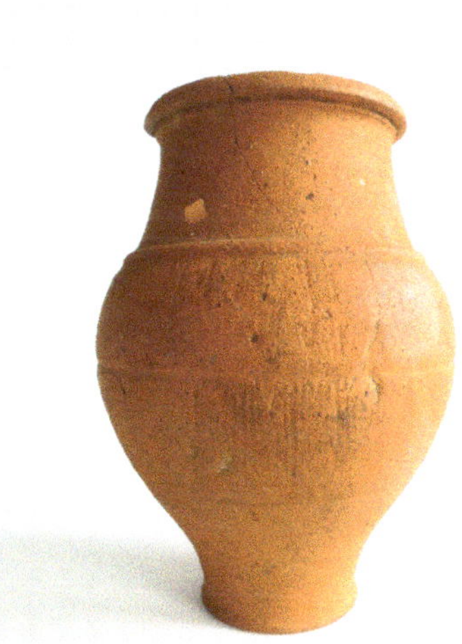

Late Iron Age/transitional vessel, found at an Iron Age cemetery in Ivinghoe, AYBCM 182.16. (Arwen Wood/BCM, 2019)

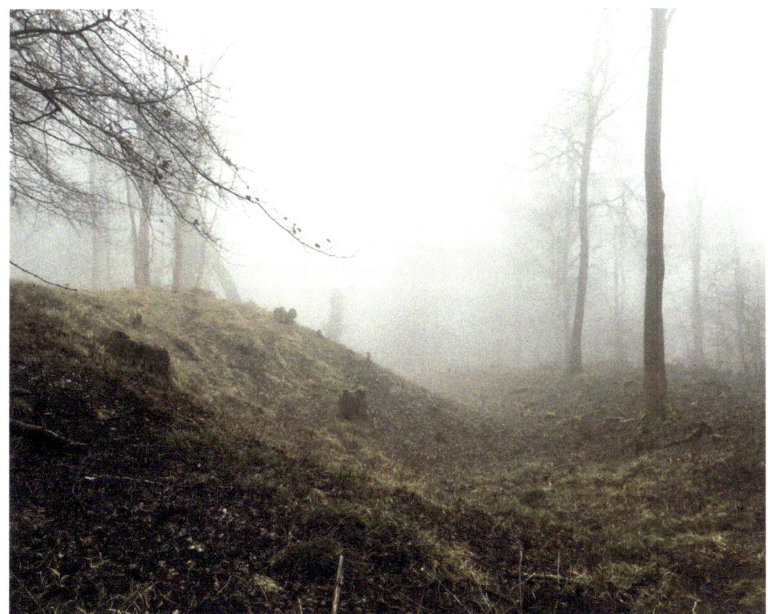

Boddington Hill Fort, near Wendover. (Arwen Wood, 2018)

An early coin of the period found in Buckinghamshire is this copper alloy potin, dating from *c*. 80–50 BC. This coin was issued by the Cantiaci tribe who were based in the south-east, predominantly the modern county of Kent, showing that coins were exchanged across the country.

Coins such as this were cast rather than struck, and still retain the casting sprues where they would have originally attached to other coins in the mould. The design on potins is very simplistic with a stylised head of Apollo, almost birdlike in appearance, facing right on the obverse. On the reverse there is the outline of a charging bull facing right, again highly stylised and devolved from the original image.

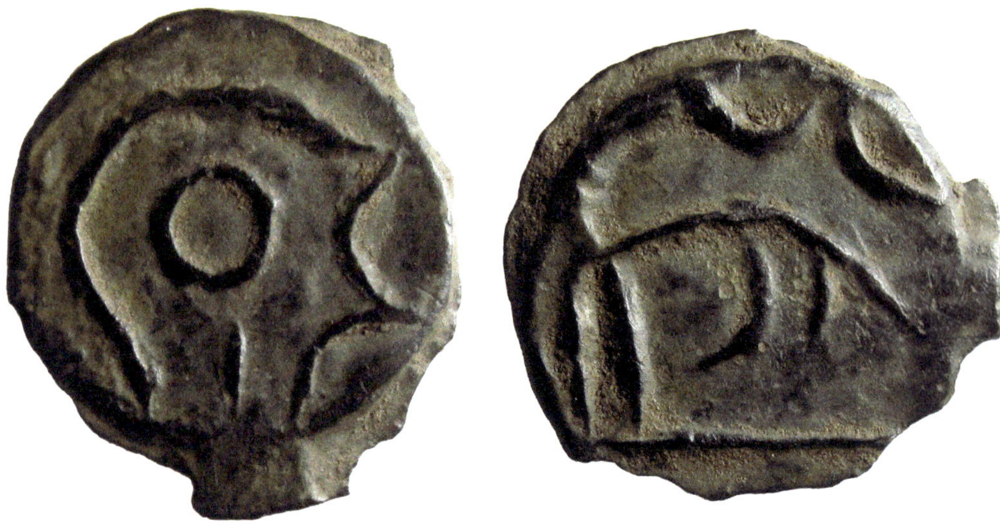

BUC-B20751, a potin.

Brooches were first used in Britain in the Iron Age and were made in both copper alloys and iron. The object would have been cast in one piece, and they were usually sprung in a similar fashion to a modern safety pin. Brooches would have served two purposes; firstly, their practical function, to pin clothing together, and secondly as a form of decoration designed to catch the eye of the viewer. Brooch types varied extremely over time and come in many different forms, with an increasing diversity into the Roman and later periods. These items would have been a form of expression for the wearer; just like today the individual would have chosen a certain design to wear. They may have expressed cultural or tribal affiliations, social status or an adherence to a deity or belief. When looking at this brooch it's easy to forget that it would originally have been a bright bronze gold colour and would have brought a vibrant flash of colour to the wearer.

Copper alloy objects tend to be a green colour when excavated because the copper has oxidised. Occasionally the metal can get a type of corrosion known as 'bronze disease', so named because the corrosion occurs beneath the surface before erupting out and flaking off the outer layers. This is very damaging for the object and is identified by a bright green powdery appearance. If found, found the object will have to be stabilised by a professional conservator to prevent deterioration and eventual disintegration.

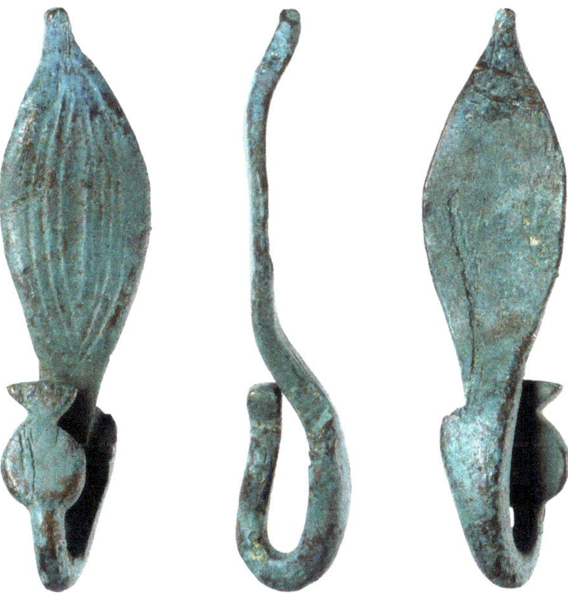

BH-9A0EEC, a La
Tène brooch.

This is an incomplete copper alloy Early Iron Age trapezoidal 'Hallstatt' razor of Jockenhövel's 'Flörsheim' type dating from *c.* 800–600 BC. The razor is trapezoidal in shape with openwork decoration and has a single curved cutting edge. It would originally have been longer, but the two bars end in worn breaks where it has broken in antiquity. At the top of the object there is a circular attachment loop indicating that originally it would have hung down from another object or been worn by a person. Less than twenty of these objects have been recorded onto the PAS database, and they are generally found in a band running from central eastern to south-west England. They are also found on the Continent in Western Europe where they have a wide distribution. A number of examples have been found as part of metalwork hoards which has allowed them to be dated alongside the other objects.

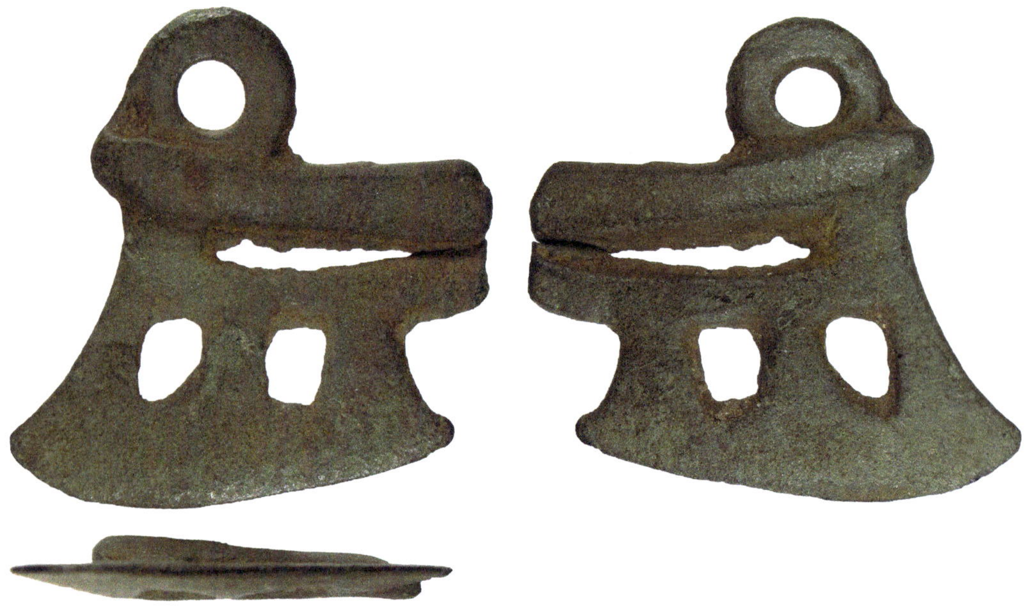

BUC-58FFF8, a Hallstatt razor.

This hoard consists of seventeen gold coins known as staters and nine silver coins referred to as units, and dates to the early first century AD. The coins were issued by Cunobelin and are types that were struck in the northern Thames area, probably in the region of Verulamium. Unusually for the period, some of the coins are inscribed with the name of Tasciovanus in the form of either 'TASCIIOVA' or '[TASCIO]VANTIS'. Tasciovanus was the leader of the Catuvellauni from *c.* 20 BC–AD 9 and is often attributed with making Verulamium the centre of his kingdom. His son, Cunobelin, succeeded him and ruled until AD 40 during which time contact with the Roman Empire seems to have increased. Cunobelin minted coins at both Verulamium and Camulodunum, now modern Colchester, after which he seems to have established hegemony over the Trinovantes and other neighbouring tribes.

Cunobelin was producing coins with his father's name inscribed on for two reasons. Firstly, to show his connection to the previous leader and to create a secure dynasty; secondly, to ensure continuity, the local population would have been familiar with Tasciovanus' coins and the association provided people with a continuation of stable rule and tradition. Coins of the Iron Age period often depicted very abstract images. Many of these coins portray the typical stylised horse on one side and a single ear of wheat on the other, while others draw parallels with Roman designs. Coins were not used for everyday transactions, instead they seem to have been used to store wealth in standard units and as diplomatic gifts between powerful rulers.

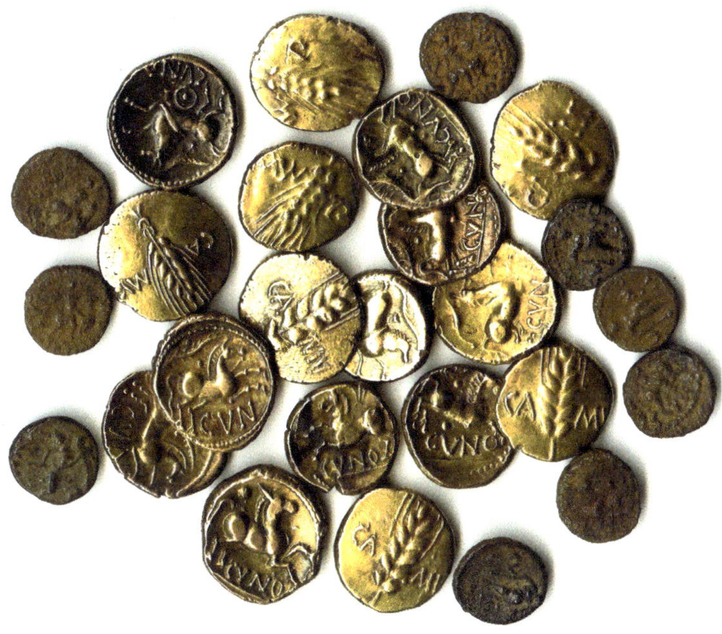

BUC-6877F8, a
coin hoard.

The design and type of many artefacts often isn't confined to a single period, but instead occur at the transitional phase between two cultures. Often traditions and knowledge continue, even when a new culture or social structure is introduced. This is true for this object, a copper alloy button and loop fastener. It is thought to date from the Late Iron Age to Roman period, with the earliest examples believed to date to around 100 BC. They continued in use until approximately AD 200. The fastener was thought to have been used to hold together a dress or cloak made from fabric, such as wool or leather. The head of the button would have attached like a button today, with a shank and loop to attach to the fabric. This example has a flat 'D' shaped head, which is decorated with a large ring and dot set at the top of a concave-sideded triangle that could be interpreted as a leaf shape. The recesses in the design may have originally held enamel, adding another colour to the bright metal. Button and loop fasteners are often found on Roman military sites in Britain but are generally categorised as being made by local British craftsmen. They are an excellent example of object traditions being carried on by the local people, but also being adapted and adopted by the Roman immigrants.

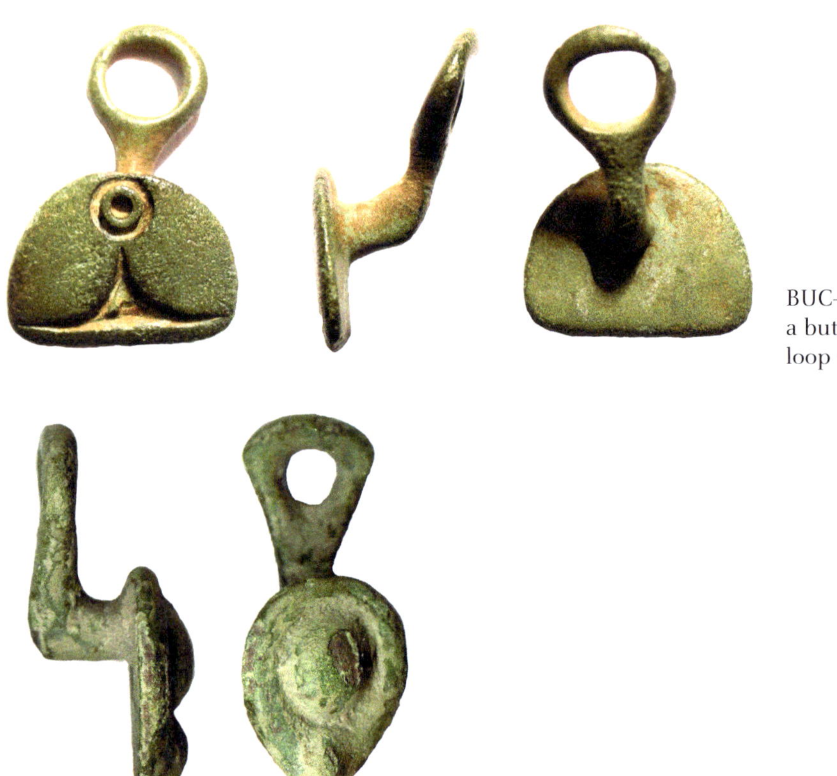

BUC-517682, a button and loop fastener.

BUC-6D3351, a button and loop fastener from Great Missenden.

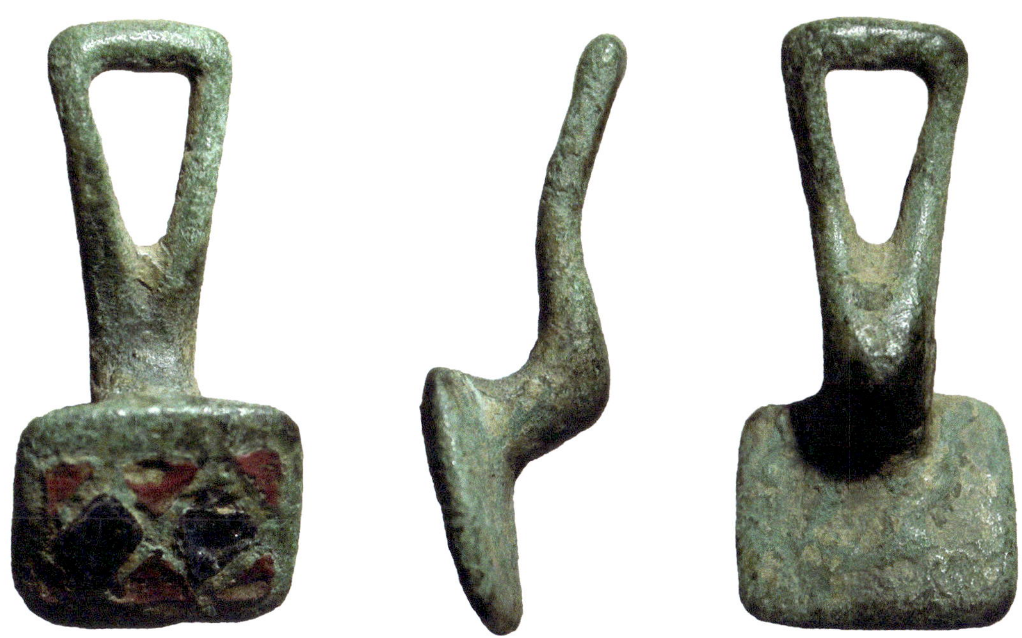

BUC-2E01A2, a button and loop fastener from Great Missenden.

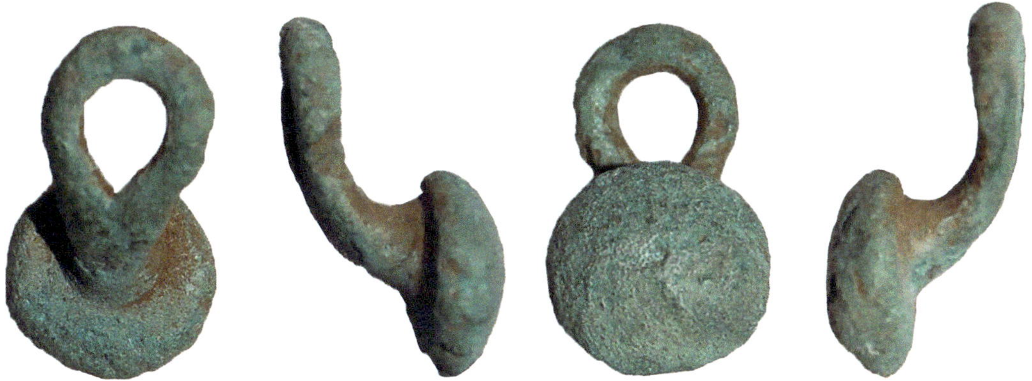

BH-5A3B42, a button and loop fastener from Bledlow.

This object is a strap union, probably from a horse harness, and is another object that dates to the Late Iron Age/Roman transition. It would have been used as a junction between two leather straps on a horse harness, perhaps relating to the use of chariots, which were common in Britain during this period. It might also be argued as being an attachment for a person's clothing, though it is quite substantial and heavy duty for this function. This type is associated with the Late Iron Age. However, another type is found only in Roman contexts, suggesting that they continued to use traditional harnesses or chariots long after the conquest.

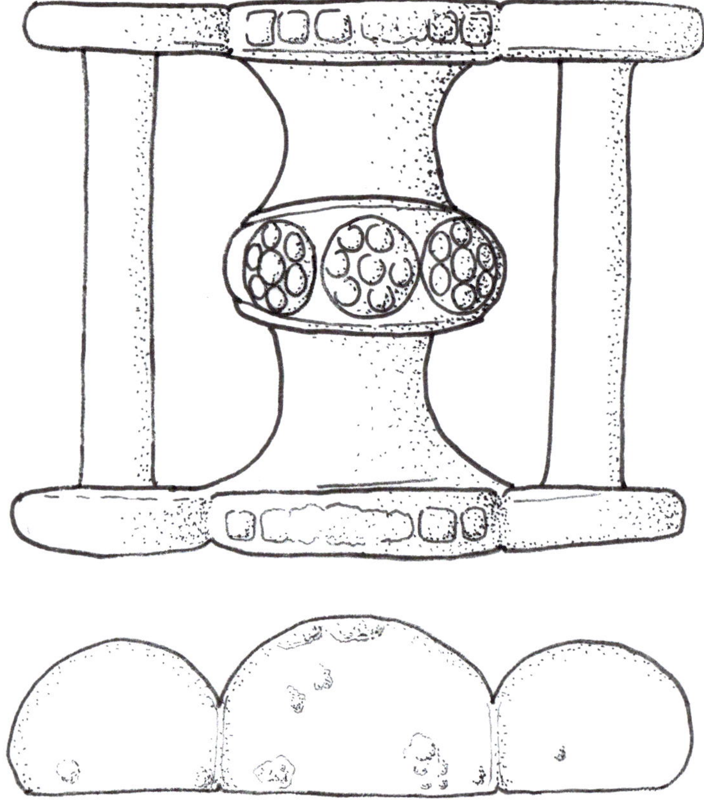

Drawing of BUC-6FF468, a harness fitting. (Edwin Wood, 2019)

Chapter 4
The Roman Period

The Romans invaded and began the conquest of Britain in AD 43 during the reign of the Emperor Claudius. While there is some debate, it is most often argued that they entered the country at Richborough in Kent and fought their way across the Thames before marching on the Catuvellaunian royal centre at Camulodunum. As detailed in the last chapter, the Catuvellauni tribe's lands were encompassed between Oxfordshire, Cambridgeshire and Buckinghamshire. Under Cunobelin they had been gaining power within the country and at the time of his death, just before the invasion, they had claimed power over much of the South East, moving their political centre to Camulodunum in Essex. With the fall of the royal centre much of the Catuvellauni surrendered and the Roman legions set out across Britain to occupy the country.

With the arrival of the Romans, settlements became more ordered with a network of roads running across the country to link them. Towns were established and often set out on an organised grid system, such as the nearby Verulamium, near St Albans. In Buckinghamshire the evidence suggests that some of the settlements continued from the Late Iron Age to the Roman period, and structures such as roundhouses continued to be built. As the Roman period progressed, however, buildings tended to change to a more rectangular shape.

One of the biggest developments during the Roman period was the system of roads built across Britain. This increased the communication and trade across the country and allowed greater movement for the military. Several of the major Roman roads cross the county. Akeman Street runs across the county from Verulamium through the roadside settlement, near Aylesbury, and towards the military fort at Alchester outside Bicester. Watling Street connects the Kent ports (including Richborough), meeting with Akeman Street outside Verulamium, and continuing past Magovinium (close to modern Milton Keynes) before ending on the Welsh borders. Evidence from excavations suggests that the roads were predominantly constructed during the first century AD and continually maintained during the Roman occupation.

While there are no major Roman towns in Buckinghamshire, with Magiovinium in the north perhaps the most substantial settlement, there are a number of smaller roadside settlements and buildings across the county, which would have catered for the more

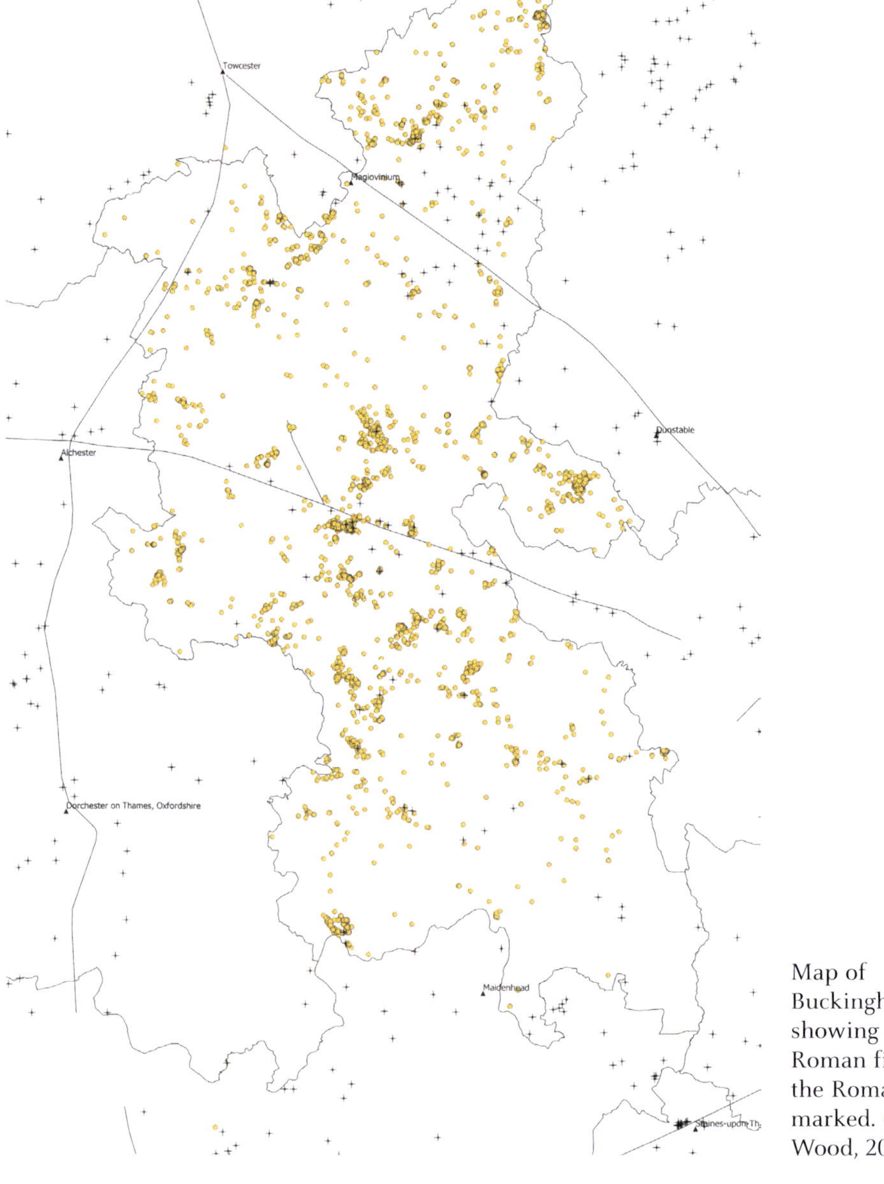

Map of Buckinghamshire showing the Roman finds, with the Roman roads marked. (Edwin Wood, 2019)

dispersed local communities and travellers on the new highways. There are some notable villas such as Bancroft villa, near Milton Keynes, and Hambledon villa, in the south of the county, and the countryside would have been dotted with farmsteads. The majority of the Romano-British population would have been simple farmers working the land and looking after their animals following the patterns of the seasons.

The Roman occupation of Britain lasted officially until AD 410, when the last of the field army was withdrawn to fight on the Continent. Although, it is likely the people of the province continued to believe themselves to be Roman and tried to maintain some semblance of a 'Roman' lifestyle for many years after this date. Certainly, as late as AD 450 provincial officials were writing to the emperor and some evidence suggests that perceptions of 'Roman-ness' endured long after the fall of the Empire in the West. The Roman period is approximately 400 years and saw great social and cultural change – the Roman soldiers who left Britain at the start of the fifth century would not have recognised their colleagues who had invaded the island in AD 43.

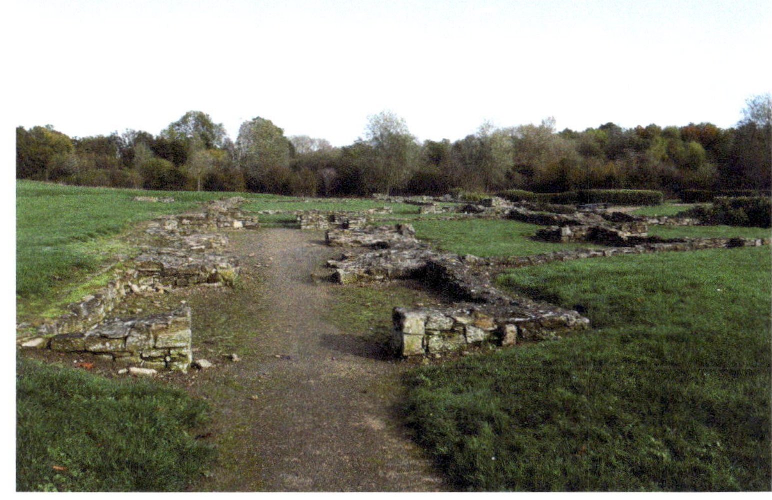

The remains of Bancroft Roman villa in Milton Keynes. (Arwen Wood, 2019)

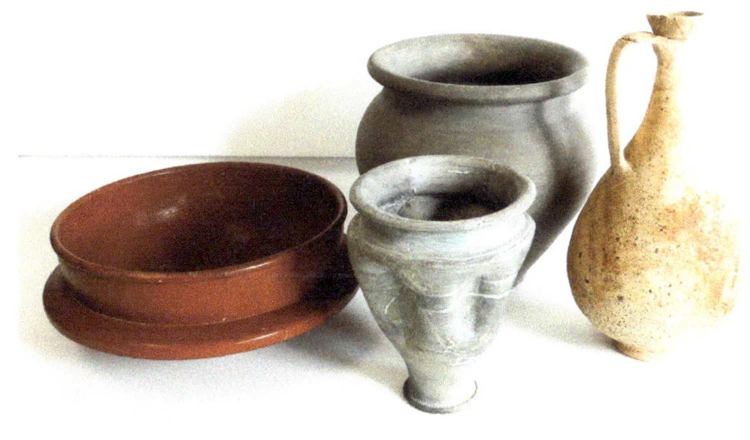

A selection of Roman pottery, from Bucks County Museum Collection, found across the county showing the variety of styles and techniques. (Arwen Wood/ BCM, 2019)

This is a coin of the Emperor Claudius called an 'as'. It is a contemporary copy dating from *c*. AD 41–54, most likely minted just after the Roman invasion. It is an unusual coin as the two sides have been copied from two different official coin issues. Contemporary copies of coins were usually made by the local community to cover any coin shortages when the official coinage wasn't available, and some coins are better copied than others. It has been argued that these coins were produced on the Continent near Boulogne to help pay the invasion force and assist in developing a monetary economy in Britain. On this coin Claudius is shown on both sides, with his bust on the right and a full portrait on the reverse of him standing veiled holding a simpulum (a type of ladle used for making liquid sacrifices). Roman coins served as imperial propaganda. By having his image on the coin Claudius was ensuring that his subjects knew who their ruler was and especially who was paying the army, thus hoping to secure their loyalty.

Roman coins are one of the most common finds brought in for recording, and demonstrate the propaganda being spread across the empire.

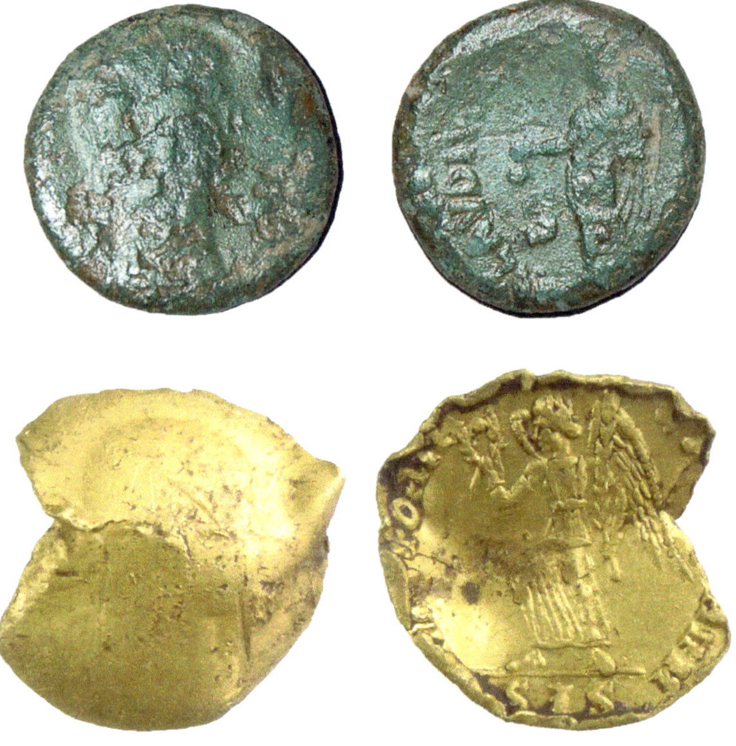

BH-F1BDDF contemporary copy of an 'As' of Claudius.

BUC-773C01, a gold semissis of the House of Constantine dating to AD 335 found in Buckingham.

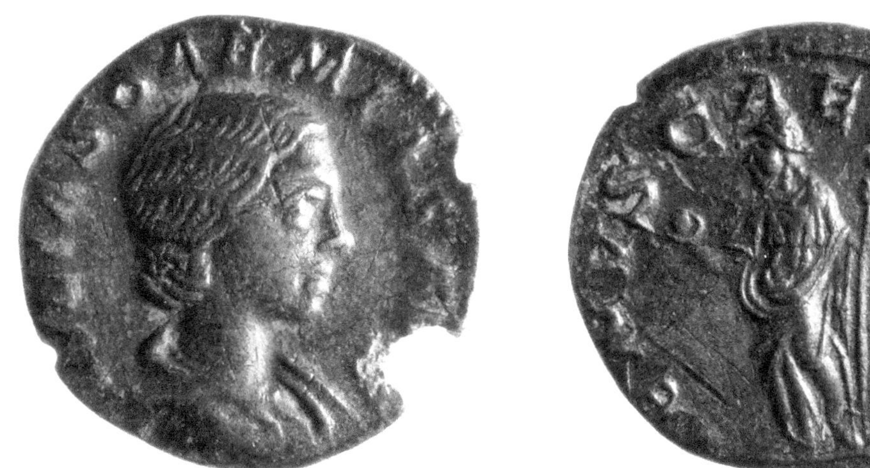

BUC-2C6327, a silver Roman denarius of Julia Soaemias dating from AD 218–22, found in Princes Riseborough.

This is the head of a copper alloy horse figurine and although the rest of the figurine hasn't been found, similar statuettes suggest that this would have been part of a horse and rider sculpture. The decoration around the mouth suggests that the horse is wearing a bridle for riding. Horses would have been an important part of transport across Britain, allowing the Romans to communicate and travel quickly across the landscape. This figurine may have had a religious meaning as a similar statuette was found on an excavation of a shrine in Northamptonshire. That example was thought to be connected to the cult of Mars or a local warrior god, and given as a votive offering. Similar brooches have also been taken as characterising a local Romano-Celtic rider god and is a good example of where Roman beliefs have possibly been integrated into the local traditions.

Horses appear to have been significant in Late Iron Age Britain, appearing on coins, as seen in the previous chapter. The expense of keeping and maintaining a horse, or indeed a team of them for a chariot, would have ensured that they were the preserve of the elite. The arrival of the Romans brought large numbers of cavalry to Britain, many of whom were drawn from the conquered Gallic and Germanic peoples of the empire. These people seem to have shared a similar association of the horse with deities and elite culture, perhaps helping to maintain these ideas in Britain.

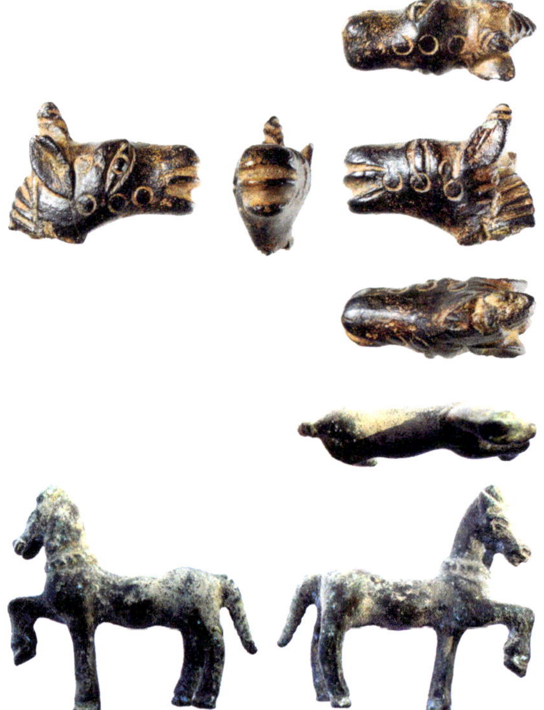

BH-9713CC, a fragment of a horse figurine.

BUC-48D9D5, a horse figurine found in Padbury.

Part of the joy of recording objects for the Portable Antiquities Scheme is the range of objects that are bought in from everyday life. This Roman knife handle is no exception, being a practical but beautiful object found in Aylesbury Vale. The handle has a large cat or panther head projecting out with its jaws open, the handle then curves round indicating the belly of the animal, before ending in a large feline paw. Folding knife handles are common from the Roman period, though the more typical design is the 'Hare and Hound', where a dog pursues a fleeing hare. These objects are both practical, folding for portability (and a possible early health and safety feature), and a work of art, displaying the skill of the metalworker.

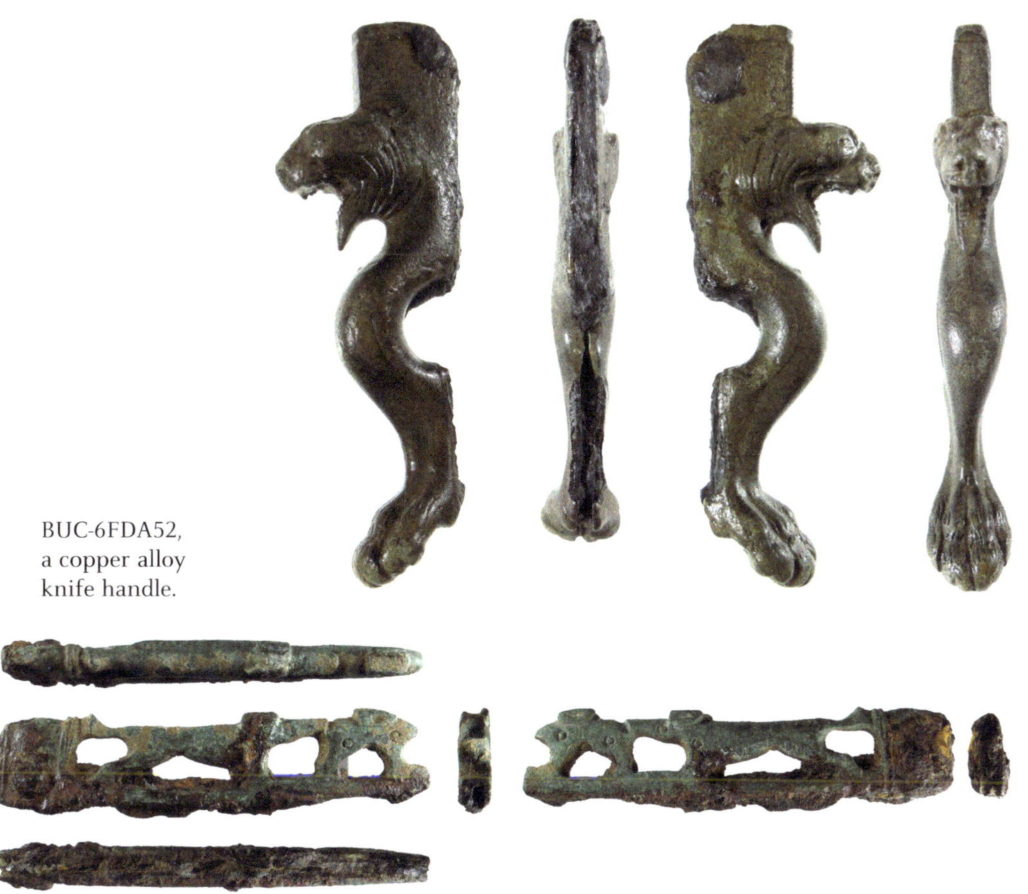

BUC-6FDA52,
a copper alloy
knife handle.

BUC-3DEC8E, a Roman knife handle of Hare and Hound type, recorded in Buckinghamshire but found across the border in Bedfordshire.

The gods and religion were an important part of Roman life. Figurines were often kept and displayed within the home and were household spirits known as the *lares* and the *penates*. These were the household gods and protected the home and the hearth. There were many gods and spirits, and the Romans identified with them and they were often representations of important aspects of everyday life. The figurine is of the Roman god Mercury, who was god of trade and commerce, and suggests that the original owner was looking for luck or fortune within their business. Mercury is naked, which is typical of how the gods are depicted. He has a cloak over one shoulder. It's not clear what was held in his left hand, but it may have been a caduceus. This is a herald's staff typically held by Mercury, which had two snakes wrapped around it and wings at the top. There is possibly a cockerel, sitting at the feet of the figure, which is another common attribute of the god.

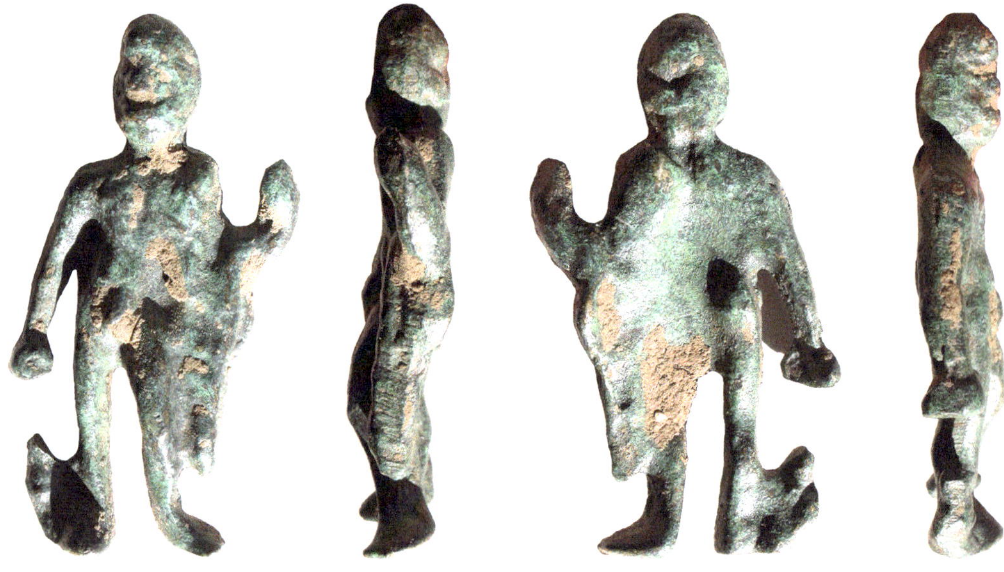

BUC-831267, a figurine.

This copper alloy mount was found with another similar mount, suggesting that they were a pair, and appear to have been cast from the same mould. Similar, smaller excavated examples have been found to be fittings for containers for cremated bone, however these ones are larger. Other examples have included door knockers from Pompeii, and decoration on wheel hubs, making this a popular decoration for the Roman period. The exact function is unknown, and it could be that they are evidence for a settlement or the remains of a now lost box or chest.

Lions are commonly used as decoration on Roman objects, and this figurine below was found close to Princes Risborough. The lion sits on a plinth, suggesting it is part of a larger object, and, like the two mounts, it may have been a decorative furniture fitting. Unfortunately, this is a historical find, so the findspot is estimated and, while it remains a wonderful art piece, its archaeological value is limited. Other common depictions of lions are found on studs, vessel mounts, fittings from furniture and indeed as the spouts from Roman *mortaria*, though some later examples look more like angry bats.

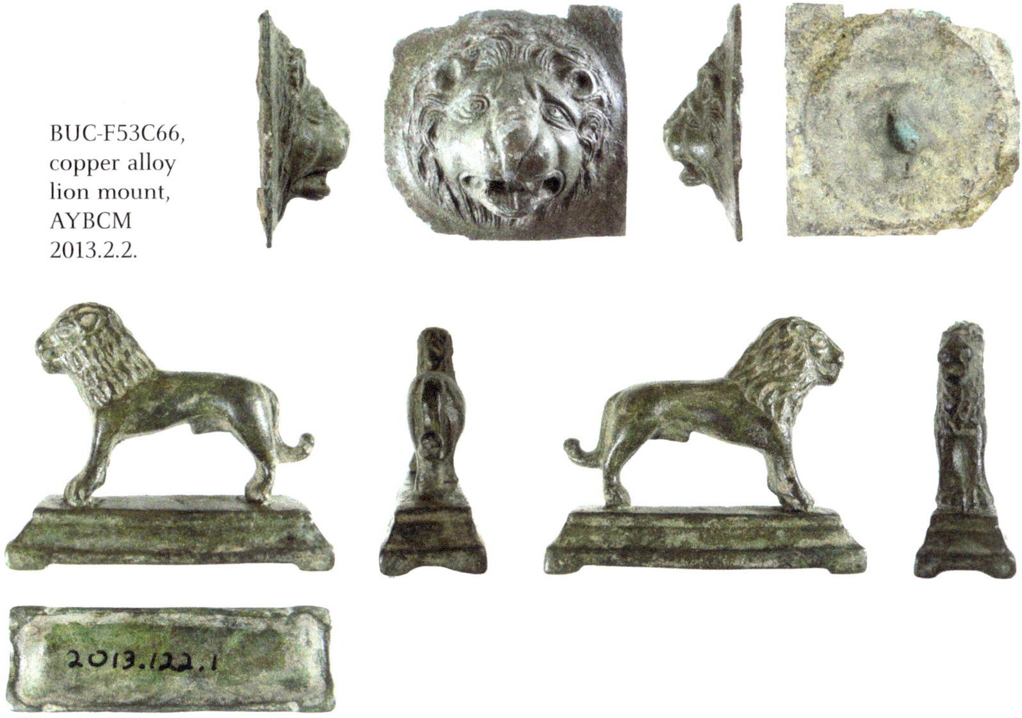

BUC-F53C66, copper alloy lion mount, AYBCM 2013.2.2.

BUC-0C7D27, a figurine of a lion found in Bledlow, AYBCM 2013.122.1.

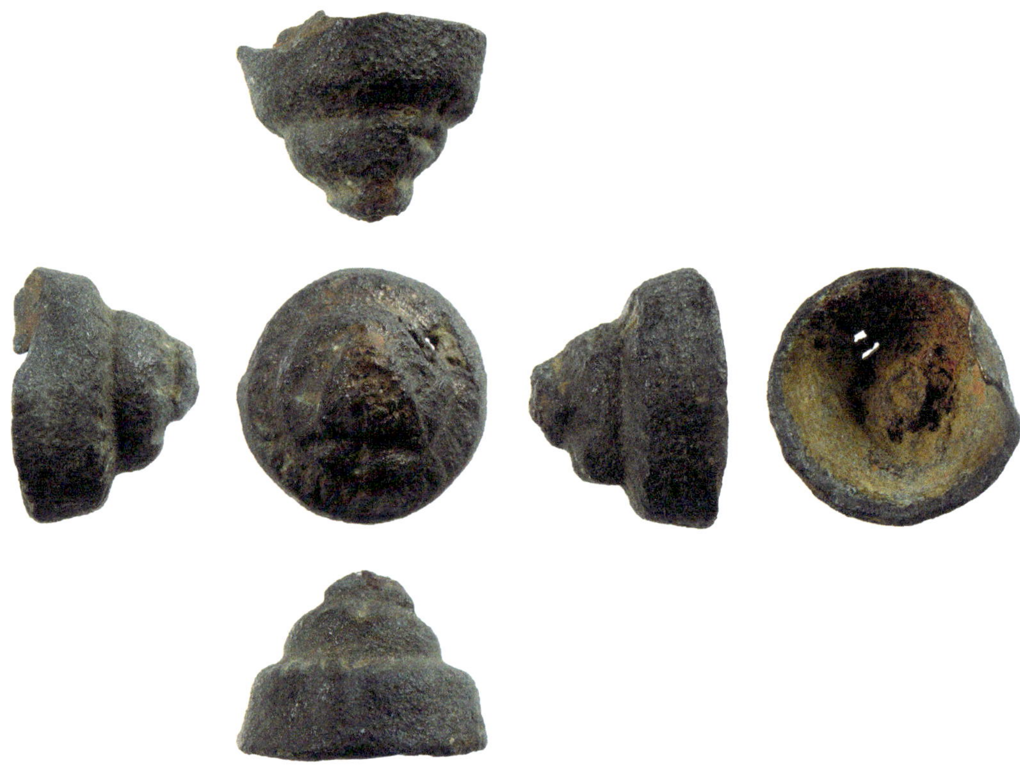

HAMP-AF74C9, furniture fitting found in Haddenham.

Roman brooches are beautiful decorative objects that had a practical use. As with their Iron Age predecessors, the brooch would have been used to fasten clothing together. It was also a personal object, and brooches from this period vary greatly in their form and decoration. This copper alloy trumpet brooch is in the form of a fly and retains traces of the enamel that was held in the wings of the insect. The surface of the brooch has a silver coating on it to give the object the impression of being made from a more expensive metal. This would have been a very decorative and brightly coloured object designed to draw the attention of the viewer. At the head of the brooch is a circular attachment loop. This most likely would have connected to a chain, perhaps strung with beads, which would have hung between this and another brooch upon the other shoulder.

Roman brooches were manufactured in many different styles, metals and shapes, such as bow and plate types with sprung or hinged pins. There are even examples that are fully three-dimensional animals, such as the enamelled cockerel brooch. This suggests personal choice was as important as practicality in deciding what people chose to wear, and certain types seem to have become more fashionable at different times. Due to this huge variety and rapid change, brooches are often used as dating evidence for sites. These are some examples of the different brooches found in Buckinghamshire.

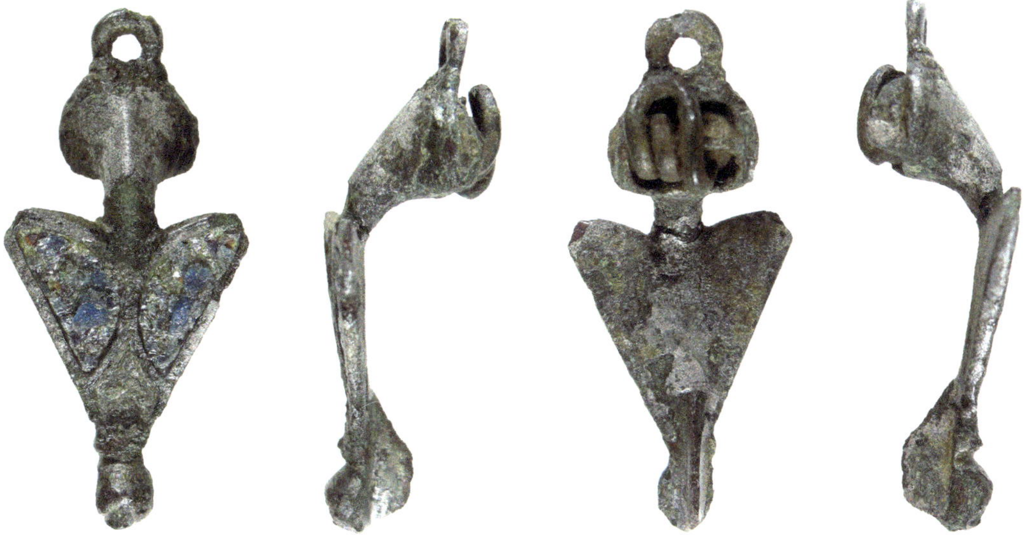

BUC-4B4741, a Roman trumpet brooch.

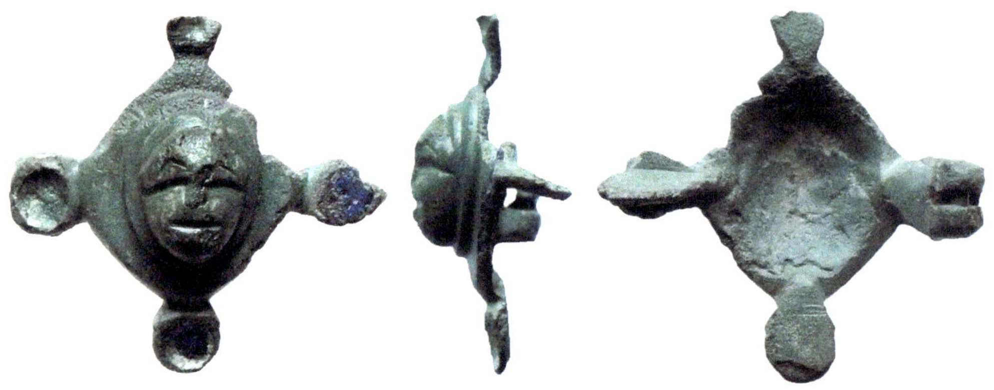

SUR-8905CD, a Roman plate brooch of probable second-century date found in Ibstone.

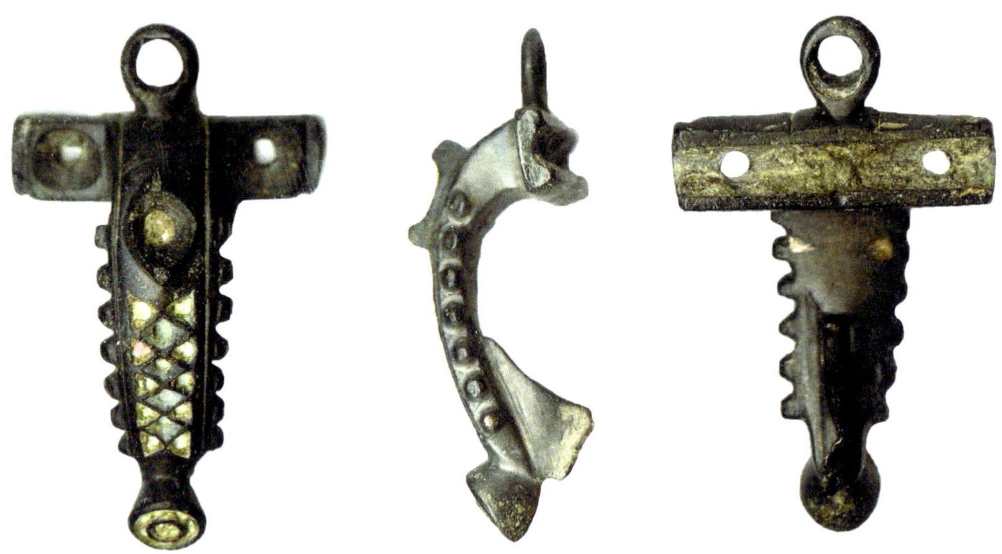

BUC- 615653, a headstud Roman brooch found in Great and Little Kimble.

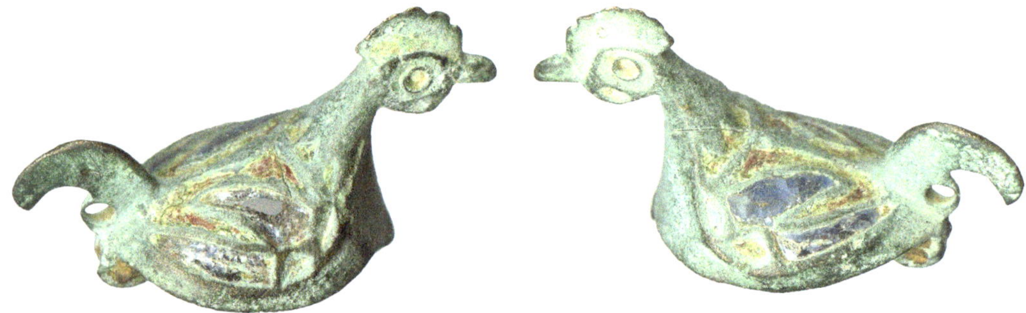

BUC-D52294, a Roman zoomorphic brooch in the shape of a cockerel, found in Chenies.

The Romans also wore other decorative jewellery, including rings, bracelets and necklaces.

This gold finger ring was found in Buckinghamshire and is quite small. This may mean it was for a child or was worn on the upper part of the finger, before the first knuckle. The band is simple, widening at the bezel, and has a raised phallus motif soldered onto it. This was a popular design used in Roman imagery and was used to ward off the 'evil eye' and bring good luck. The image of the phallus is used on brooches and pendants, such as this pendant found in Thornton. Roman finger rings came in a variety of metals and designs, some of which also held stones or enamel decoration as can be seen in the images below.

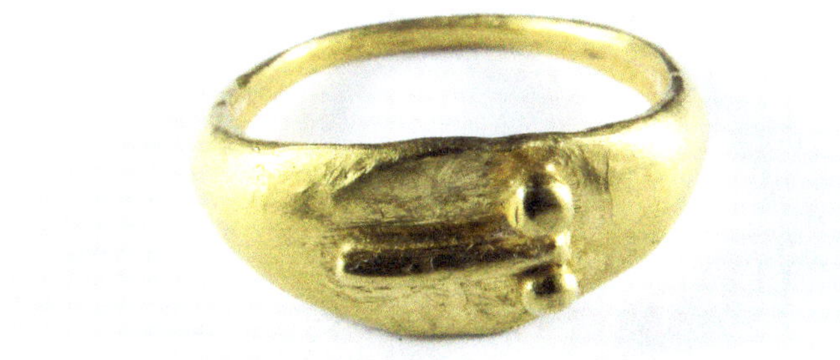

BUC-C9CEE4, a
gold finger ring
AYBCM 2014.10.1.

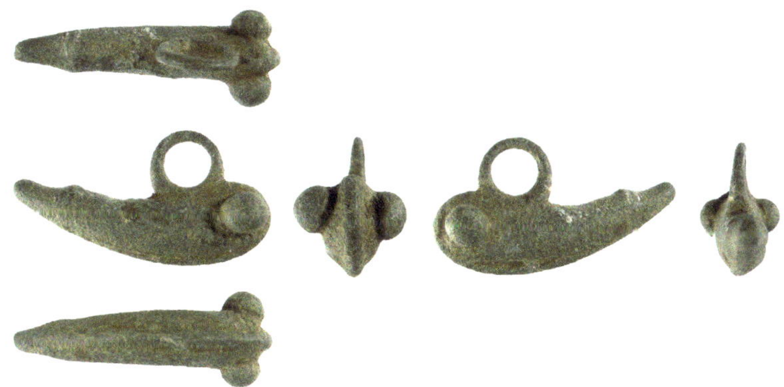

BUC-4E8D7E, a
phallic pendant
found in
Thornton.

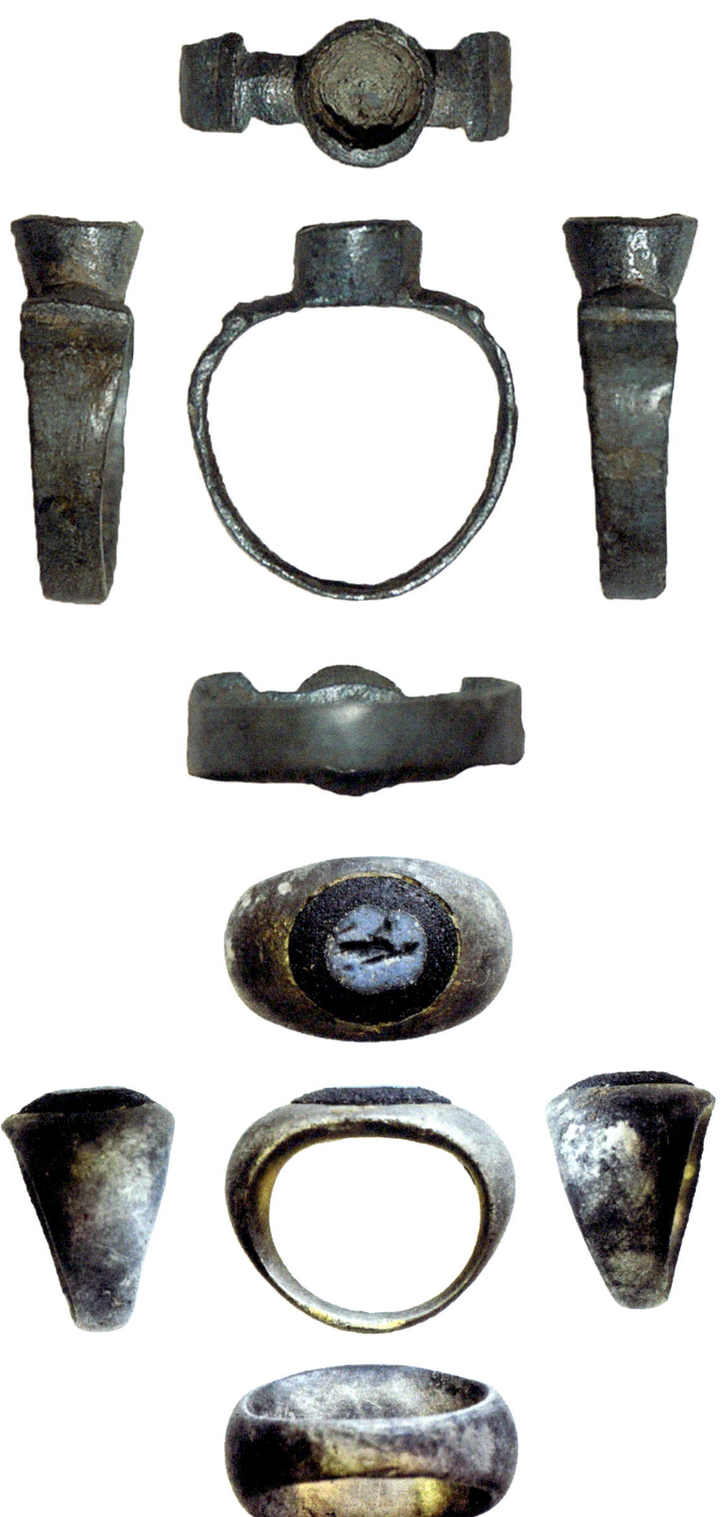

BH-16632E, a copper
alloy finger ring
found in Bledlow.

NARC-C23DF1, a
silver finger ring
with blue intaglio
bezel found
in Hanslope.

The end of the Roman period is officially regarded as AD 410 in Britain. However, as mentioned earlier, it transitioned gradually into the early medieval period. This buckle is an artefact from that period and is dated from AD 350–450. It is Hawkes and Dunning type IIC and is decorated on the face of the frame with a continued pattern of punched ring and dot design. The buckle would have been attached to a leather strap which would have attached through the smaller hole, the lack of decoration indicating the area that would have been hidden.

These buckle types are thought to be associated with the late Roman military, and it is interesting that they were found in Buckinghamshire. The county has no known military sites or forts dating to this period, though this may be due to the billeting of troops within civilian settlements to ease the burden of supply on the military. Examples of these buckles and other military associated finds from throughout the Roman occupation are often found as single finds within roadside settlements, farms and villas as well as in towns and other civilian areas. These types of buckles came in a variety of designs, including this buckle and plate found in Quainton with two horse heads projecting outwards from the outer frame. Other varieties feature stylised dolphins.

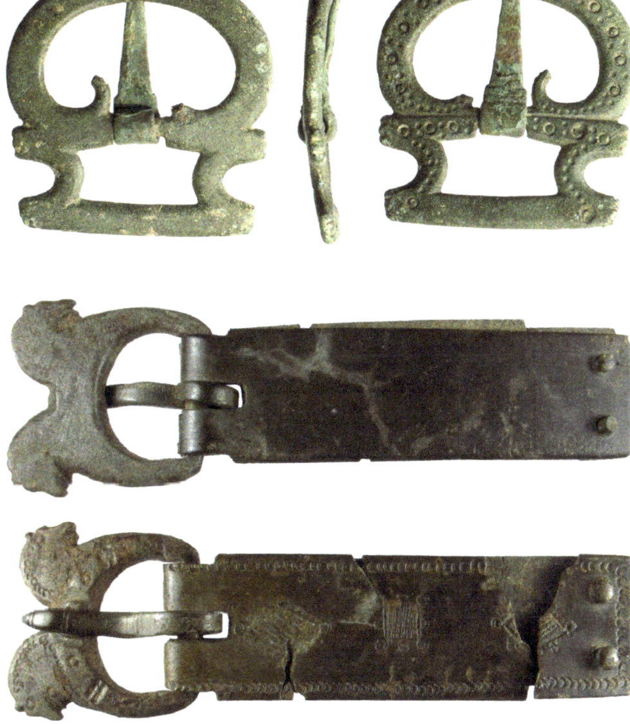

BH-7FCB64, a copper alloy Roman to early medieval buckle.

BUC-E114D2, a copper alloy buckle and plate dating from AD 350–450, found in Quainton.

Chapter 5
The Early Medieval Period

The collapse of Roman authority in Britain from the early fifth century began with Roman troops being withdrawn by usurper emperors to fight on the Continent. As the century progressed there were increased attacks by raiders from outside the empire and without support from the central government Britain descended slowly into a chaotic state. This left the island open to new settlers and the Angles, Saxons and Jutes moved across from regions in Denmark, the Netherlands and Germany. Initially these groups came as raiders but then began to settle the coastal areas of Britain before pushing further inland, up the Thames Valley. Many of the finds and sites from this period tend to be in the east and south-east corners of the country, with an initial decline in evidence from the west and north.

The early part of this period is poorly understood. Roman-style objects are still found in use alongside newer objects, perhaps reflecting the incoming Germanic Anglo-Saxon culture. One example of this comes from a burial found just across the border near Bisham in Berkshire. The burial was found by detectorists and included grave goods, such as a Continental copper alloy hanging cauldron and two spearheads, also of Continental type.

The Grave also contained a copper alloy bowl similar in design to late Roman vessels produced in the later fourth century and in post-Roman Europe. Its presence suggests that links with the previous culture and with the Continent still existed and certainly the association of Rome with political and military power remained long after the empire had gone. Pierced Roman coins are also found in burials, used as jewellery, and the Sutton Hoo burial contained a number of objects made in the Eastern Roman Empire, which survived long after the fall of the West. Cemeteries and burials from this period can cause some problems with metal-detecting, due to the grave goods found within them, as it is illegal to disturb human remains without a Burial Licence issued by the Home Office.

During this period, communities and settlements contracted and the population of the island dropped. However, it is from this period, particularly the latter end, that the landscape begins to take on a shape and pattern that would be familiar to us. The early medieval period marks the beginnings of the parish system and by the end of the period most communities had a church at their heart. This is in part due to the arrival of missionaries, such as St Augustine sent by Pope Gregory in AD 587.

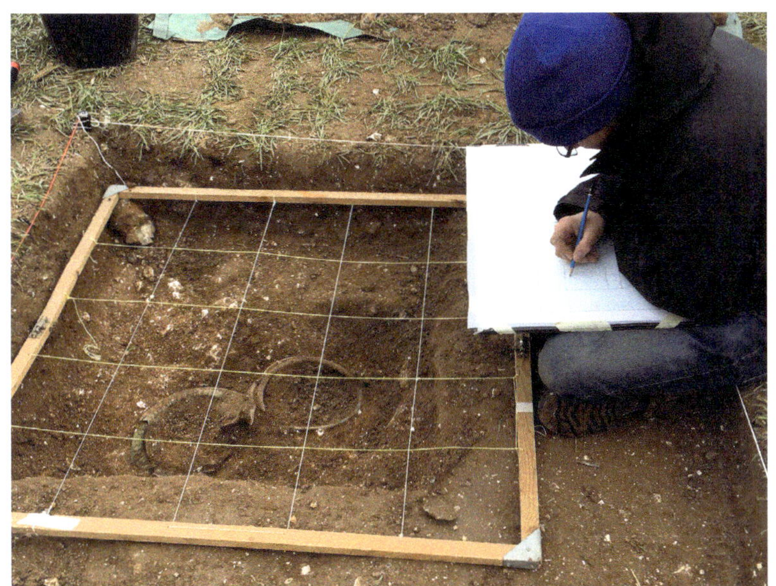

The Bisham assemblage in situ. (Arwen Wood, 2018)

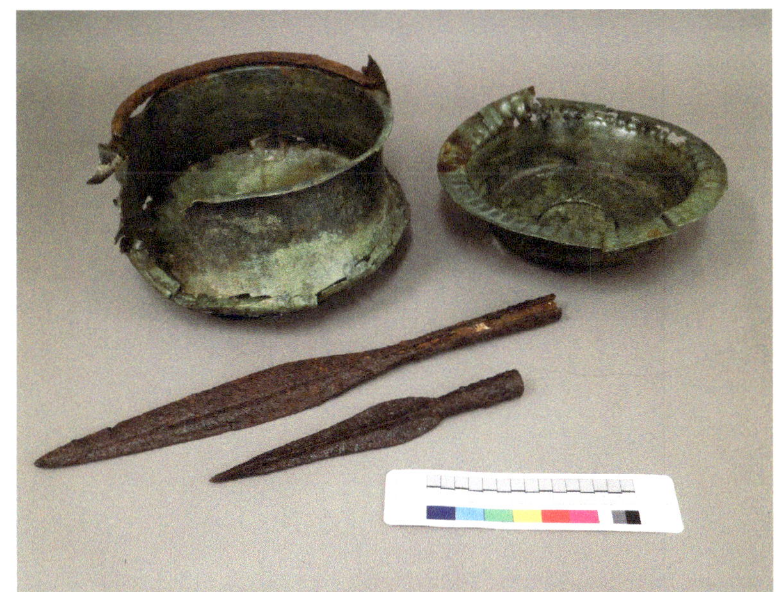

The Bisham assemblage after conservation. (Drakon Heritage and Conservation, 2018)

Many of the place names that are used now across Britain refer to this influx of people. Sussex and Wessex for the South (and West) Saxons, and East Anglia for the Angles. Indeed, the name of this county, Buckinghamshire, owes its origins to this period, Buck- coming from the personal name 'Bucca', -ing- referring to 'the people of' and -ham meaning an enclosed piece of land or meadow. Thus, the county name means literally 'the enclosed meadow of Bucca's people'. New settlements were often set up away from the earlier Roman ones, as in London where the new site of Lundenwic was set up west of the earlier Roman Londinium on the Strand and Covent Garden. It is from the ninth century that most of the old Roman towns are reoccupied.

It is a time of mass unrest, with the chaos of the post-Roman period, the violence of the Viking raids and the warfare that accompanied the formation of modern England. However, it is also a time of influence and ideas being brought in from different cultures and people, and the creation of vibrant artworks such as the treasures from Sutton Hoo or the Lindisfarne gospels. This makes the finds from the period extremely varied with different styles, art forms and beliefs all enriching the material culture of the period.

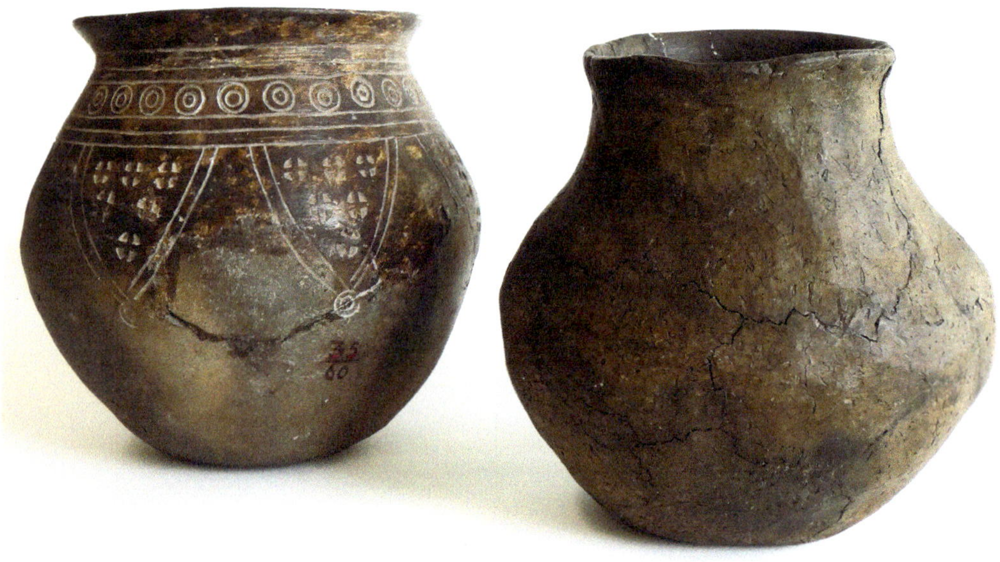

A selection of early medieval vessels, found in Buckinghamshire, from the museum collection. (Arwen Wood/BCM, 2019)

These are fragments of an early medieval brooch found by two different people but thought to be from the same brooch. However, the central part is still to be found. Known as a great square-headed brooch, due to the large square plate at the head of the brooch, it would have been completely gilded when new, though much of this has been lost after centuries in the earth. This type of brooch dates to around AD 500–570, early in the period, and it's interesting to see how the development of the brooch style has changed and become more elaborate compared to the Roman bow and plate brooches. These types of brooches are often found in female graves positioned on the shoulder of the deceased. This suggests that the brooch was worn on the shoulder, possibly to hold a piece of clothing such as a cloak in place. Other types of brooches that appear in this period include equal-armed brooches, strip brooches, small long brooches, disc brooches and saucer brooches, which are often found in pairs on each shoulder of the wearer, most likely to secure clothing. These two pieces have been donated to Buckinghamshire County Museum.

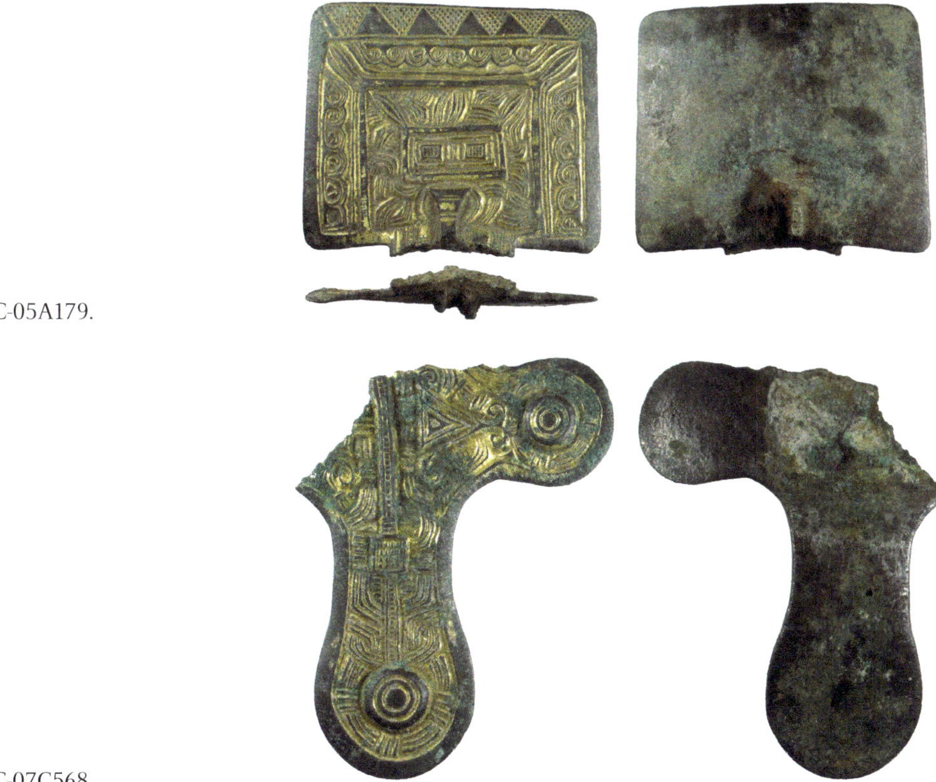

BUC-05A179.

BUC-07C568.

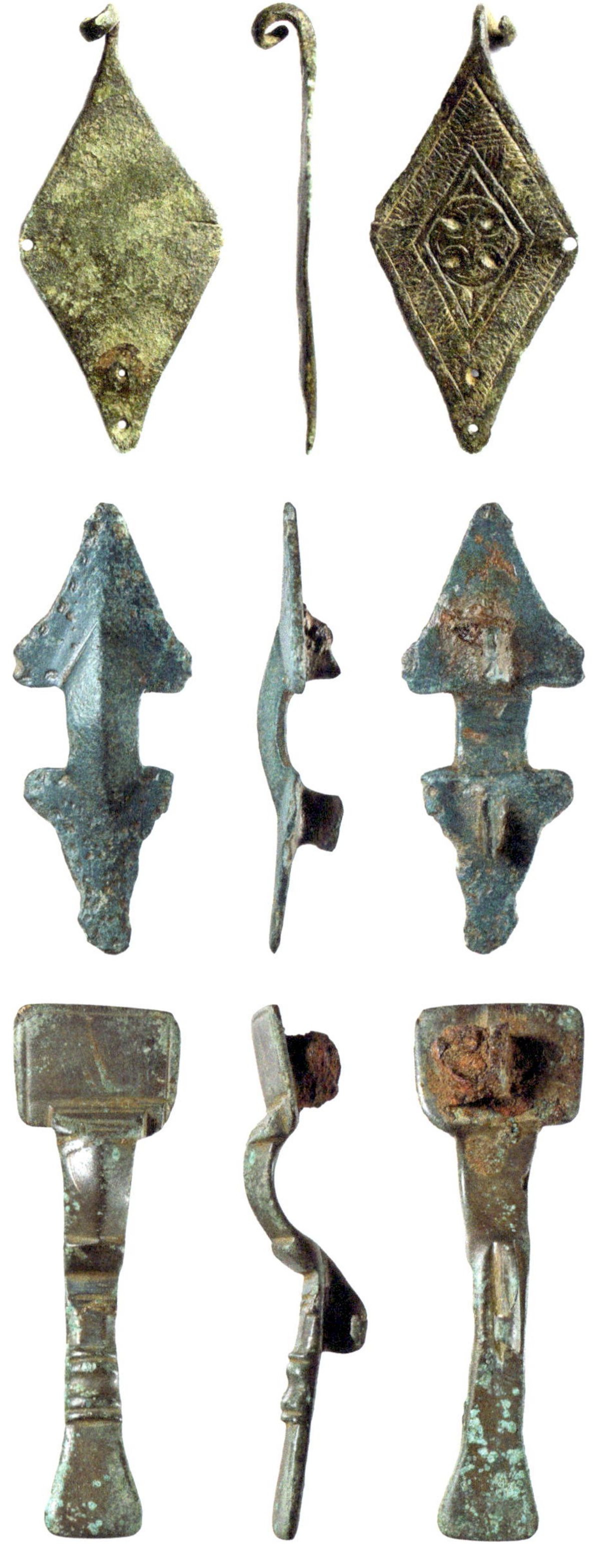

BUC-4D849D, a strip brooch found in Quainton.

BH-825EB9, an equal-armed brooch found in Longwick-cum-Ilmer.

BH-5A6AD5, a small long brooch found in Kingsey.

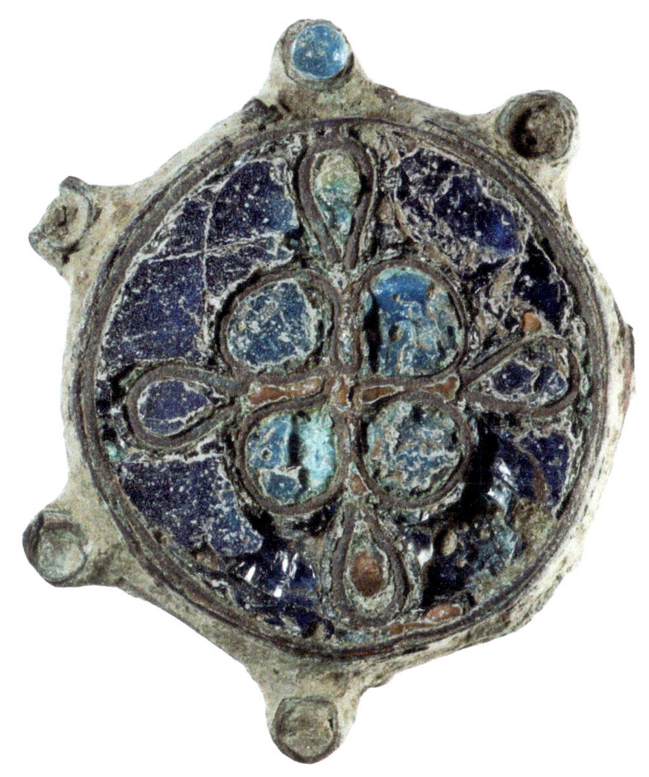

BH-2A6BB6, a
cloisonné-enamelled
brooch found in
Princes Risborough.

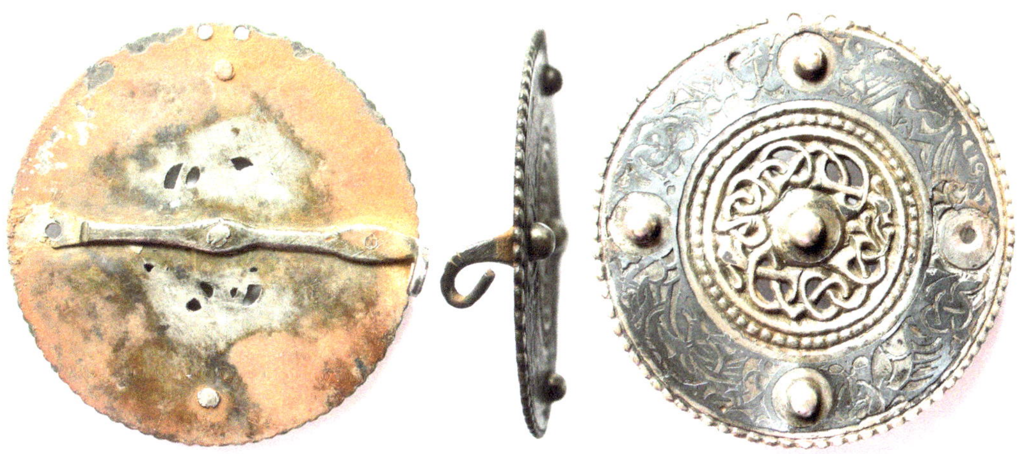

BUC-ABA063, a silver disc brooch found in Nash.

The Lenborough Hoard was found in December 2014 and excavated in situ by the previous FLO Ros Tyrell. It is one of the largest Anglo-Saxon coin hoards to be found in Britain and was found to contain 5,248 silver pennies and two cut silver halfpennies all contained within a lead parcel. The lead had been folded over and pinched closed to prevent the coins from falling out.

Once the coins were identified it was found to contain 985 coins of Aethelred II who ruled from AD 978–1016, while the rest of the coins were found to be of his successor Cnut who ruled from AD 1016–1035. The dating of the coins found that there was a gap of ten to fifteen years between the latest of the Aethelred II coins and the earliest of the Cnut coins, as none date from Cnut's earlier reign. This may suggest that originally there were two separate containers containing the two groups of coins. However, this was not revealed in the excavation.

The coins were found to have been minted all over the country and included some from Dublin, which was a Viking trading port, and Buckingham. The reasons behind the deposition of such a large collection of coins remains unclear, though the most prominent theories include it being hidden under threat, or for storage of wealth.

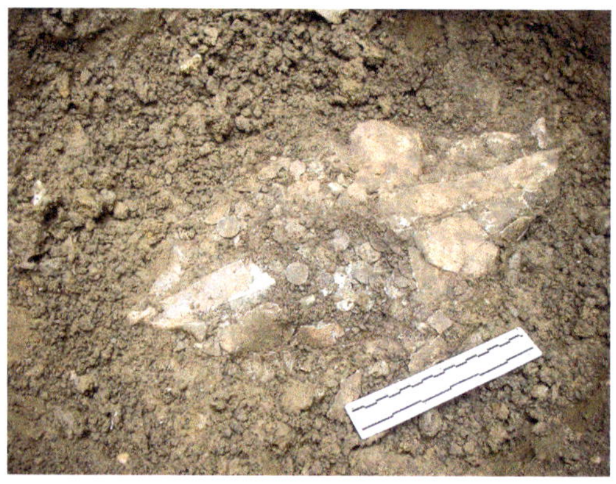

Lenborough Hoard in situ. (Ros Tyrell, 2014)

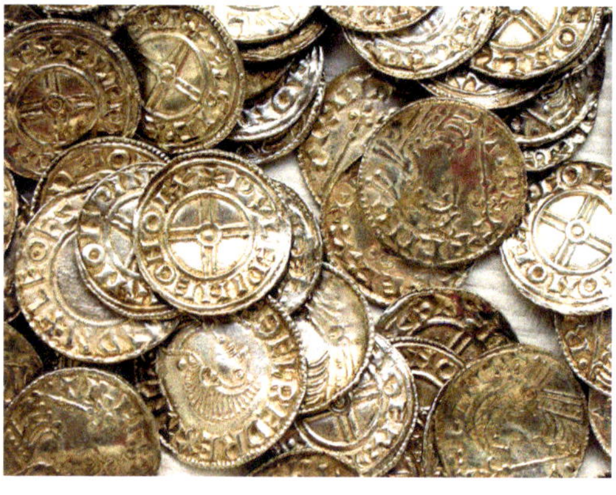

A close up of some of the coins after cleaning. (Ros Tyrell, 2014)

Coins in the early medieval period are very varied and their style changes greatly over the period. The earlier pennies or 'sceats' are more illustrative and stylised in their designs to the more standardised coins which come in later. The later ones tend to include inscriptions of the ruler and the mint where the coin was struck, as well as the names of the moneyers responsible for producing them. By looking at the different types of coins across this period the development of the style of coins used today can be seen. These coins were all made by being struck between an upper and lower die inscribed with the designs.

The Lenborough Hoard was declared treasure by the coroner and acquired by Buckinghamshire County Museum, where it is now on display.

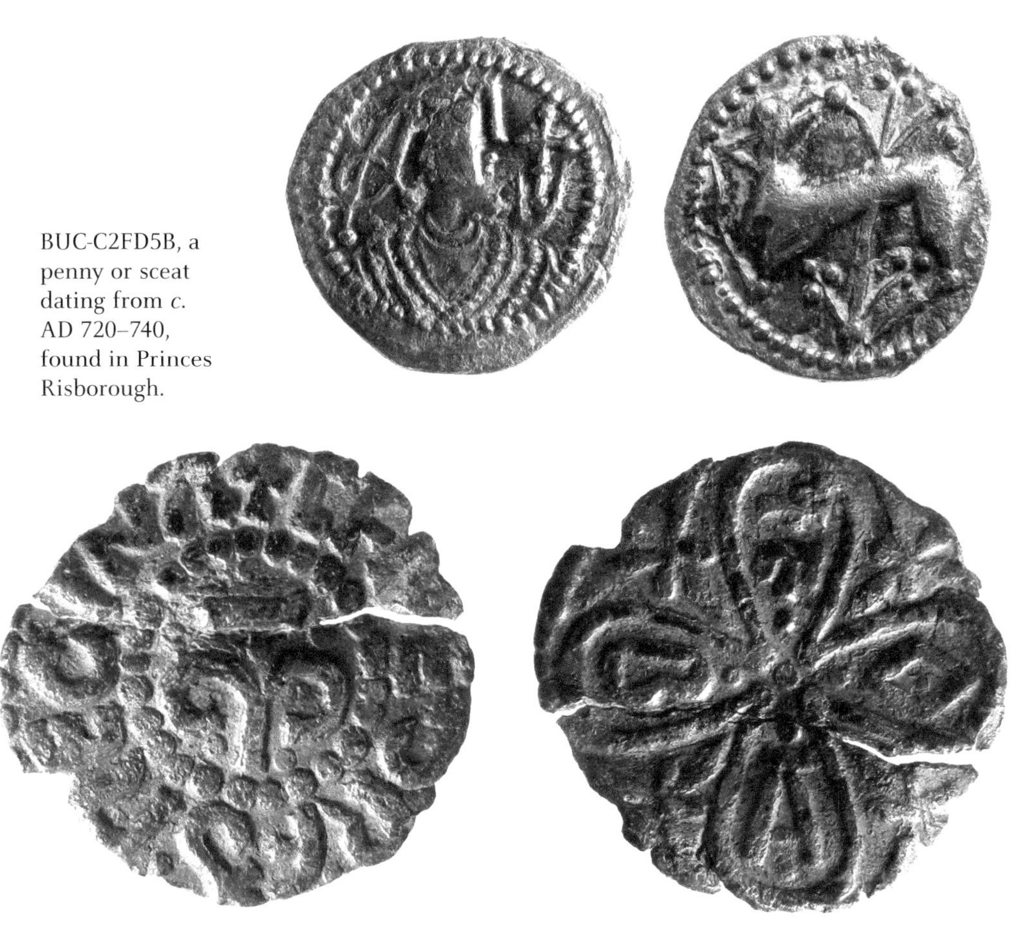

BUC-C2FD5B, a penny or sceat dating from *c.* AD 720–740, found in Princes Risborough.

BUC-C28B07, a penny of Cynethrith, wife of Offa, dating to AD 757–796, found in Princes Risborough.

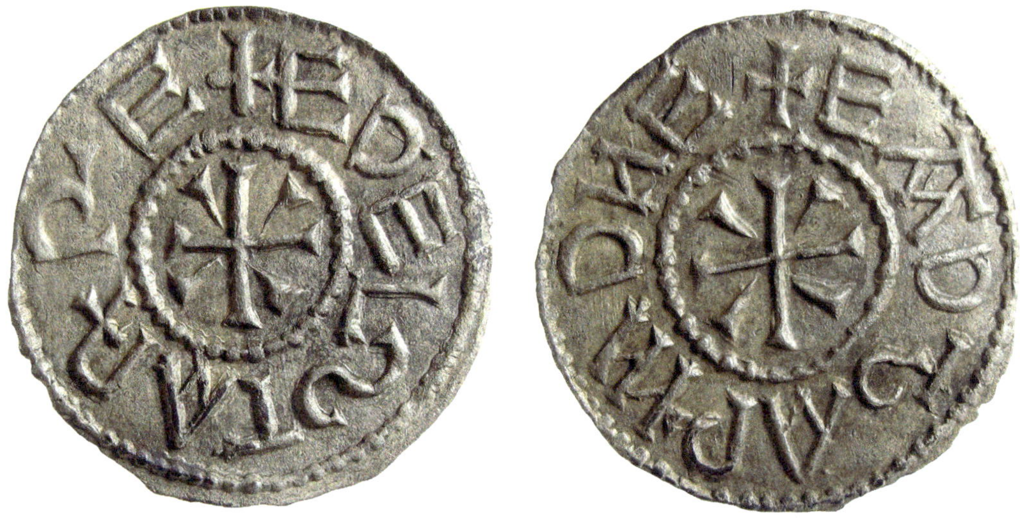

BUC-5E1D33, a silver penny of Aethelstan I dating to *c.* AD 837–45, found in Thornton.

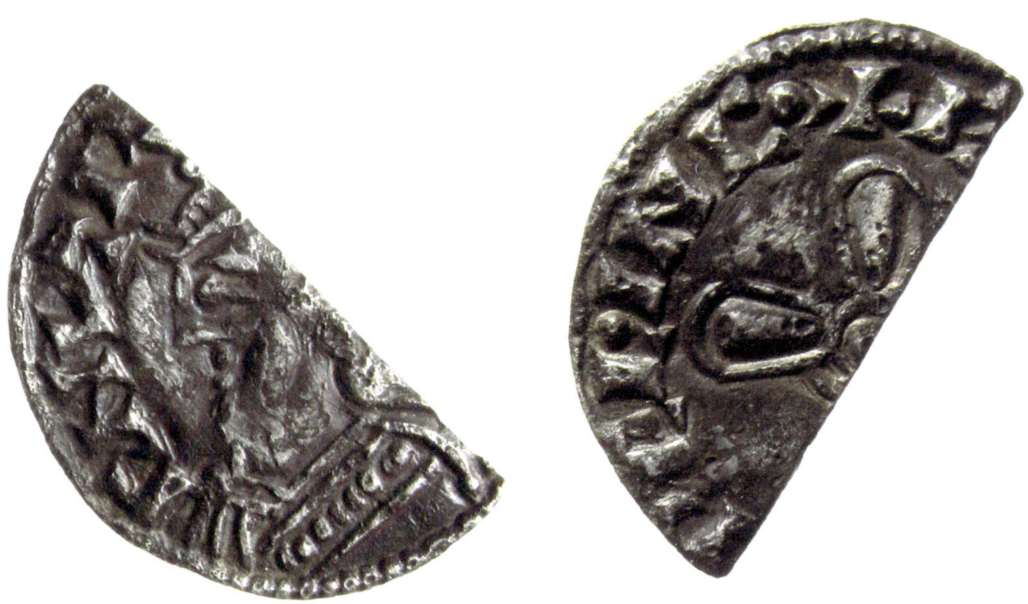

BUC-2EA283, a silver cut halfpenny of Harthacnut dating to AD 1036, found in Tyringham and Filgrave.

Occasionally objects are found that are part of the manufacturing process, rather than the finished items. These objects can be used to indicate centres of production and the technical processes involved. The decoration on this die has been deeply incised but does not have channels for liquid metal to run through, indicating that this was used as a stamp rather than a mould. The stamp is believed to be for making preßblech foils for small decorative pieces, such as brooches or leather mounts.

The technique involves the die being pressed into the metal sheet and transferring the motif or pattern within the die. This method of transferring a design can be used on a range of metals including gold, silver and copper alloy. Much like the dies used for coins, this die would have been struck with a hammer to transfer the image onto the sheet metal. It is thought this stamp was used for button brooches, which date from the late fifth to the early sixth century AD. Button brooches are found in southern England, are small or 'button sized' and are decorated with anthropomorphic face-masks, the designs are similar to faces seen on some sceats.

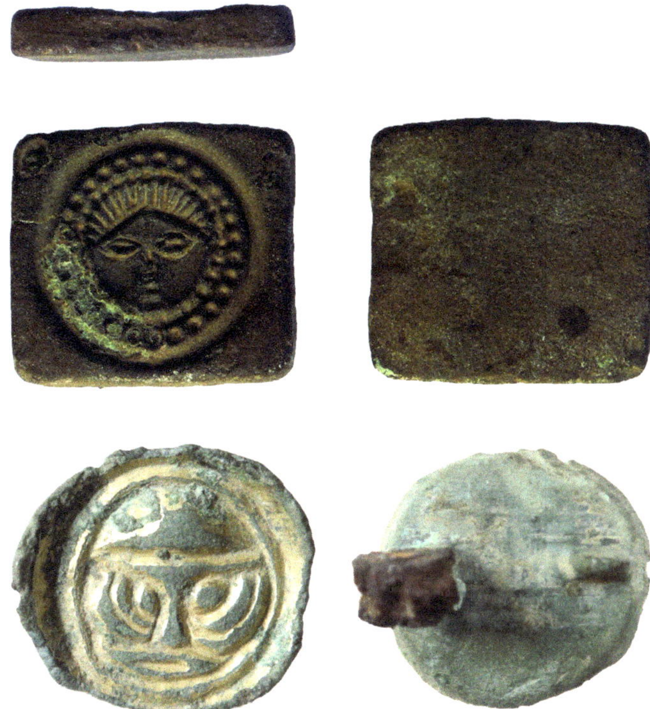

SUR-073AC0, a die stamp.

HAMP-E987F2, a button
brooch from Hampshire.

30. BUC-A2D047 Gold Bracteate
Found in Hambledon in 2005

A bracteate is a plate of thinly beaten precious metal, in this case gold, which has been made into a disc. A beaded wire border has been soldered around the rim, and a suspension loop has been made from a small sheet and attached to the edge. The disc has been decorated with a repousse design of a stylised running horse – the jaws are open, the ear is raised, and it has a round wide eye. In front of the horse is a snake-like creature, which the horse seems to be biting. These pendants originate in Scandinavia, however Continental examples tend to include a human head within the design. It is thought that this bracteate is a local imitation with the snake replacing the human head. These objects tend to be found in burials and were likely worn by women on necklaces. Bracteate pendants often are decorated with zoomorphic designs, patterns, or crude imitations of coins. This object was acquired by Bucks County Museum.

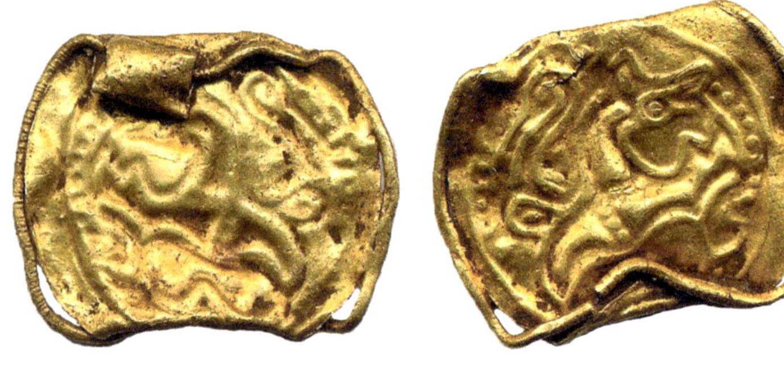

BUC-A2D047, a
gold bracteate.

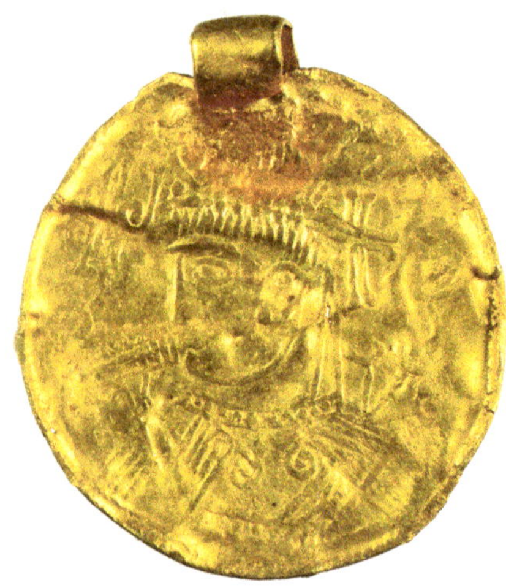

LEIC-EDD980, found in Leicestershire.

31. BUC-215ED8 Early Medieval Mount
Found in 2007 in Haversham with Little Linford

This copper alloy mount is thought to date from around the eighth to tenth century AD and is decorated with a design typical of the period featuring an intertwined animal. The head of the animal has sadly been worn away, though they are usually elongated with prominent eyes and ears, as with the horse in the previous object. The body is stylised and formed using swirled and curved shapes to create the body, legs and clawed feet of the creature. In the early medieval period although objects were used for practical day-to-day tasks, they were often beautifully decorated, suggesting that there was an aesthetic value to these objects as well. It is thought that this mount was part of a horse harness, and feasibly the decoration could relate to this. Another zoomorphic mount can be seen in the following image and is also thought to be part of a horse harness fitting. Like the previous example this was found near to Milton Keynes and is thought to date to earlier in the period, showing the longevity of style and form in these objects.

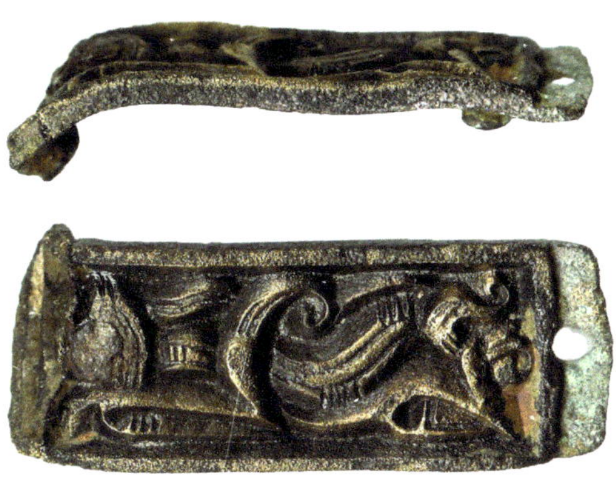

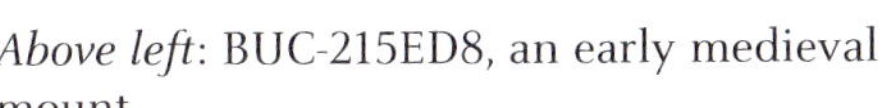

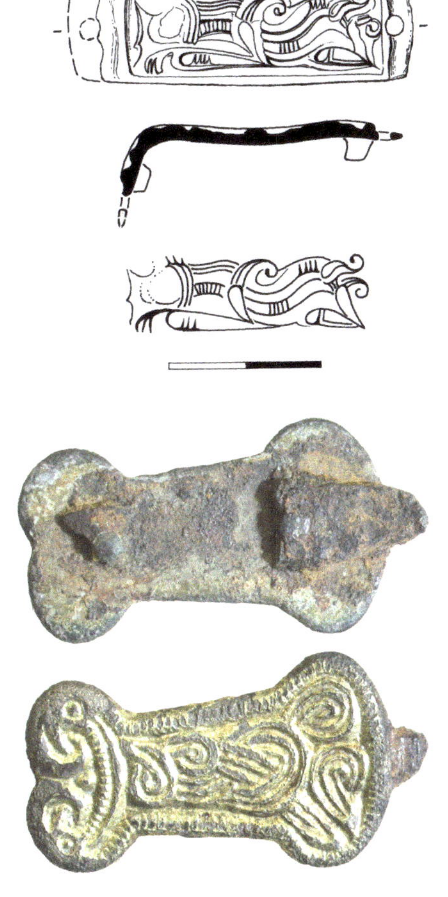

Above left: BUC-215ED8, an early medieval mount.

Above right: Drawing of BUC-215ED8.

Right: BUC-251708, an early medieval mount dating to AD 600–700 found in Little Linford.

Pyramid mounts date from the early seventh century AD and were thought to be scabbard mounts. It is now thought they were mounted on straps in pairs at the top of the scabbard to secure the sword within. These straps are often called 'peace straps' or bands, as they are thought to have been used to tie the sword into its sheath when entering a building as a gesture that no violence was intended. The mounts are often found as accidental losses and are rarely found as grave goods; however, examples have been found at Sutton Hoo. The mounts have been found made from copper alloy and other precious metals. Other parts of the sword were also decorated including the pommel, which fits to the bottom of the hilt, and the guard, which separates the hilt from the blade.

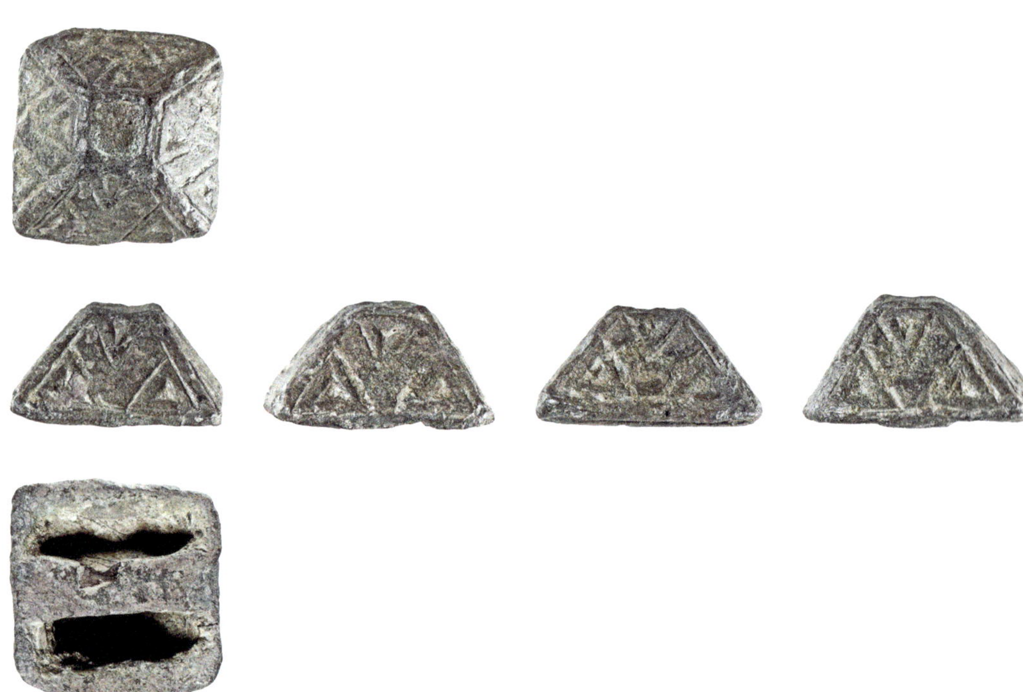

BH-40414E, a pyramid mount.

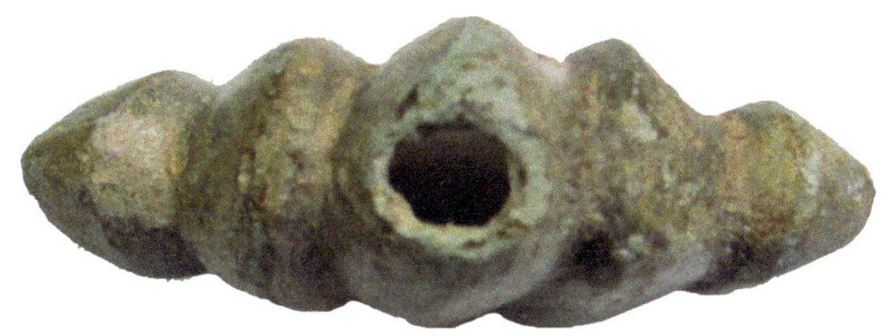

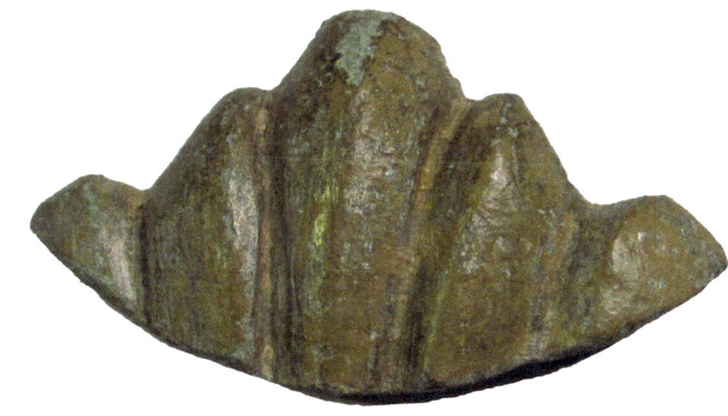

BERK-4E7837, a sword pommel dating from the tenth to eleventh century AD, found in Kingsey.

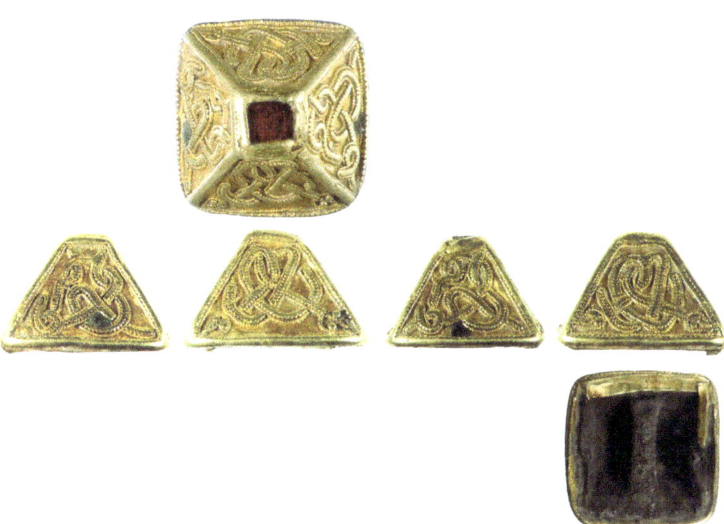

BUC-87B54A, a copper alloy with gold sheeting pyramid mount dating to the early seventh century, found in Hampshire.

Many of the objects that are brought in for recording onto the database were for personal adornment and would have been used for both practical and decorative reasons. These are personal objects, much like the jewellery and fastenings that are worn today. This silver strap end is both functional and decorative and would have attached to the end of a strap, weighing it down and preventing the end from fraying. It is of Anglo-Scandinavian type and demonstrates the similarities and eventual fusion of cultures that occurred through contact with the wider North Sea world. Other personal objects found in this period include hooked tags used to secure clothing such as leg wraps.

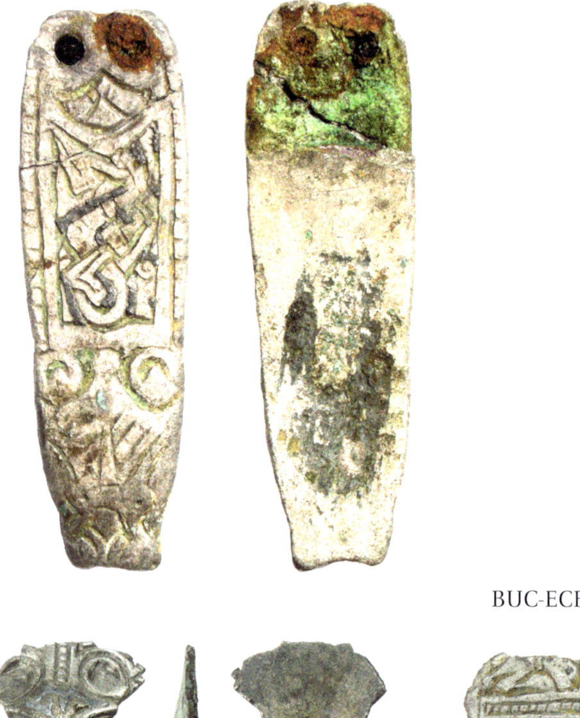

BUC-ECB33B, a silver strap end.

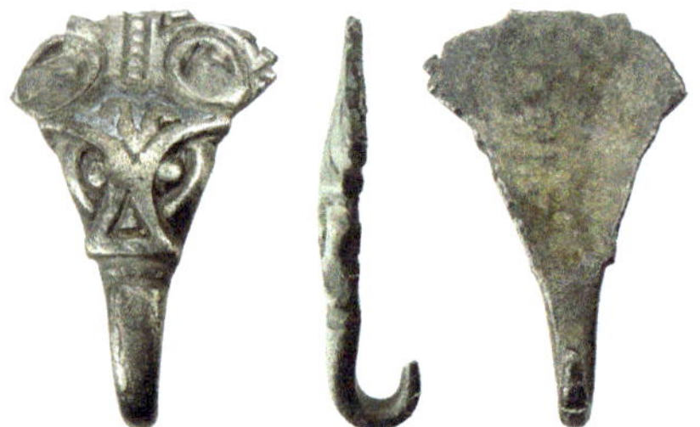

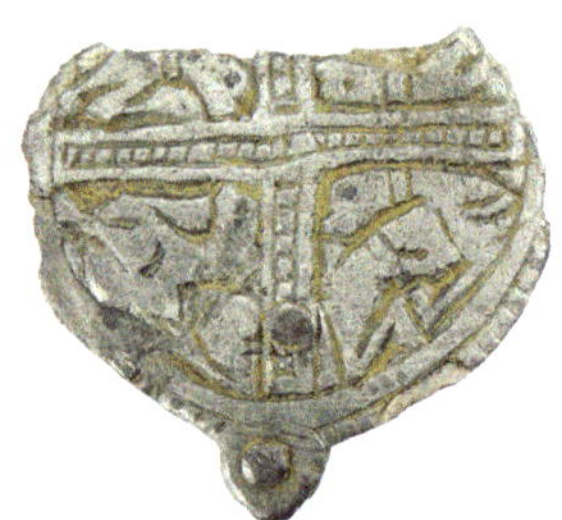

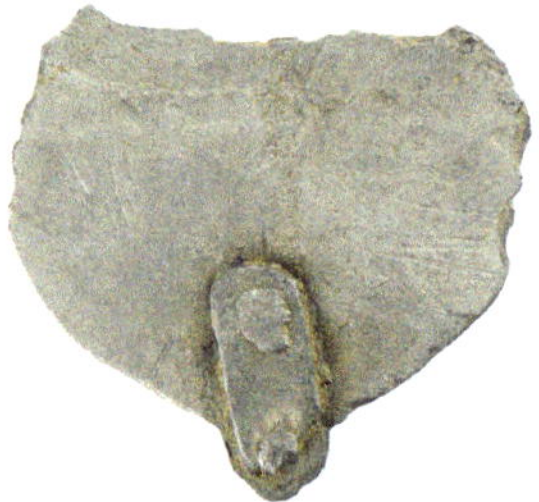

Above left: BUC-52DE42, a hooked tag dating from AD 800–1100, found in Wycombe.

Above right: BUC-7D52D5, a hooked tag dating from AD 800–950.

The horse continued to be an important part of life, as in earlier periods, providing transportation and highlighting the status of the rider or owner. Horses appear in art and decoration as on the previous objects and the objects that adorned the animals can be equally decorative, as with this last object. This copper alloy mount would have been part of the stirrup, sitting at the junction of where the leather strap hanging from the saddle attached to the stirrup. Again, this is a practical object which has been highly decorated, in this instance with a lion like creature; its head twisted back and jaws open. Other parts of the early medieval stirrup have been found in Buckinghamshire, including the terminal mounts from the lower corners of the stirrup. This stirrup mount dates from the very end of the early medieval period in the eleventh century AD and is Williams' Class A Type 11.

BUC-79B784, a stirrup mount.

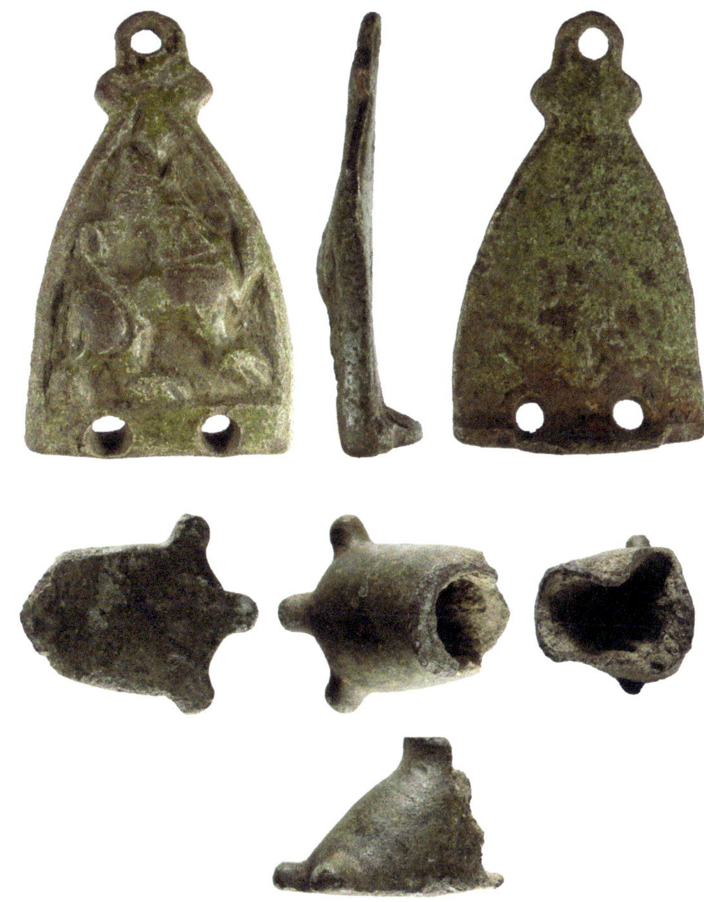

BUC-92974C, a terminal fitting dating from the eleventh century AD.

Chapter 6
The Medieval Period

In AD 1066, Anglo-Saxon England was brought to a bloody end by the Battle of Hastings and the Norman invaders, led by William the Conqueror, ushered in a new era. William's victory over King Harold Godwinson is seen as the start of the medieval period, though as before beyond the political sphere change was slow and subtle. The Domesday Book is an important record of this period and demonstrates that by around AD 1086 the familiar societal and economic frameworks of medieval England were established. The estates of the previous period were formed into the manorial systems, and the parishes were shaped from the minster church lands. The social structure of this period was based around the feudal system, with the wealthy lord of the manor owning lands that were worked by the local Anglo-Saxon population. The manorial system divided up and organised the landscape of the county into a number of estates.

The boundary of Buckinghamshire is thought to originate in the eleventh century and was probably the area designated to provide troops for the defence of the town of Buckingham. It is thought that there may have been a castle at Buckingham, and there is the remains of a motte and bailey castle at Ellesborough, though no stone castles remain standing within the county.

Typical features of this period include market towns, villages and monasteries which came to own vast tracts of land and property. Farming and fishponds, which were often part of a manor house site, have left their mark on the landscape. Medieval fields would have been open, and evidence for ridge and furrow ploughing can be seen across the county. In AD 1348, the Black Death reached England causing devastation on a scale not experienced before and leaving an enduring permanent mark on the very psyche of the nation. It is probably in part responsible for some of the approximately eighty abandoned medieval village sites in Buckinghamshire. Settlements shrank and were abandoned as one third to half the population of England died in the eighteen months the plague lasted. However, it has also been found that cultivation was in retreat well before this as a series of poor harvests caused by the 'mini Ice Age' of the mid-fourteenth century took their toll.

Many buildings in Buckinghamshire villages still stand from that date in the late medieval period. These are timber-framed buildings that would have belonged to wealthy peasants, manorial officials or were built as communal spaces to serve the needs of the village, and date from the late thirteenth century. Most village churches date from this period, though a great many have been altered over time, particularly in the nineteenth century.

It is in this period that the production of material culture finally returns, and surpasses, the levels seen in the Roman period as attested by the sheer number of finds recorded by the PAS. These artefacts represent the detritus of everyday life, with buckles, brooches, coins, jewellery and ceramics again produced on a large scale.

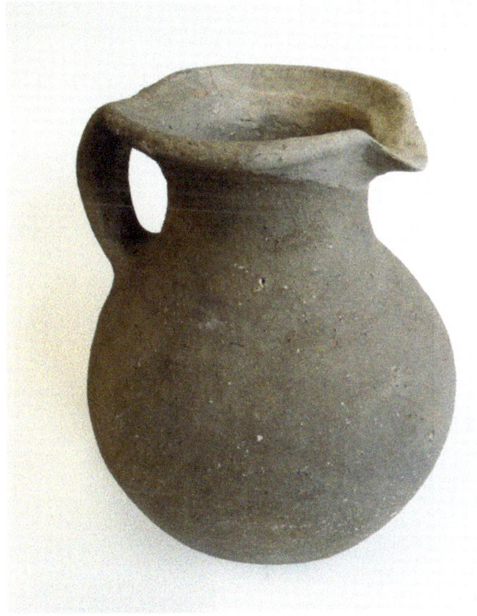

A thirteenth-century jug from Buckingham Street, Aylesbury, AYBCM 1963.3.8. (Arwen Wood/BCM, 2019)

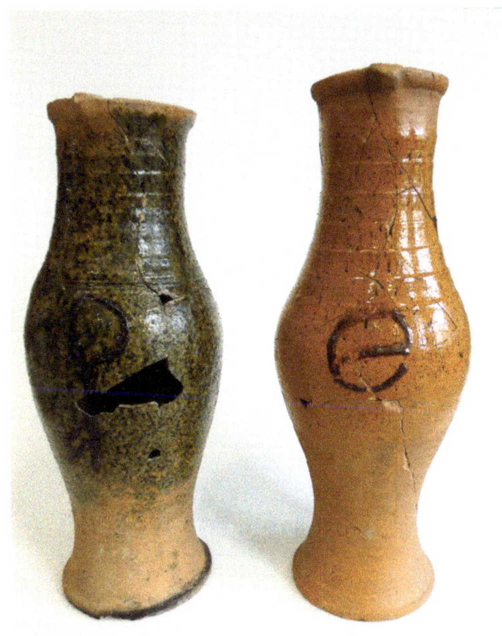

Thirteenth- to fourteenth-century jugs. (Arwen Wood/BCM, 2019)

Religion was a very important aspect of the lives of everyone in this period, and this is reflected in the range of devotional objects found. This object is a lead ampulla dating from 1350–1450 and was used to hold holy water collected from a religious site, most likely by someone on a pilgrimage to a shrine. Originally the ampulla would have had suspension loops on both sides, so it could be worn on clothing or round the neck as a visible symbol of the pilgrim's journey and devotion. The top is open and has been pressed together to prevent the contents from being spilled, others may have been sealed shut with wax. On one side of the lower chamber is a crown with a large *fleur de lis* rising from the centre. On the other side is a scallop shell, the symbol of St James of Compostela and also that of pilgrimage – scallop shells were often used as early pilgrim badges. It also appears on the badge of the town of Reading, whose monastery held a relic of St James and would also have been a centre of pilgrimage. Ampulla are often found in rural locations in the middle of fields, and it has been suggested that they were deliberately emptied and ploughed into the soil to bless the fields. Bradwell Abbey in Milton Keynes was founded in AD 1154 and was a place of pilgrimage to the chapel of St Mary. It is a local site which was affected greatly by both the plague and poor harvests.

Other objects such as the papal bulla on page 74 show connections with the Continent, which were strengthened by the Catholic Church and increased international trade. The bulla would have been used as an authentication seal on official papal documents sent out from Rome and features the faces of St Peter and St Paul, as well as the name of the reigning Pope. Other objects found across the county include pilgrim badges, crosses and depictions of the Holy Trinity. Objects such as these represent the dedication to religion that infused every aspect of life, but also a very personal sense of hope and prayer for the individual.

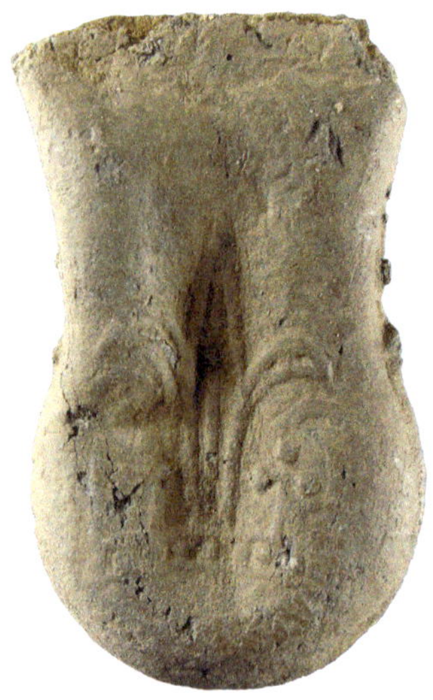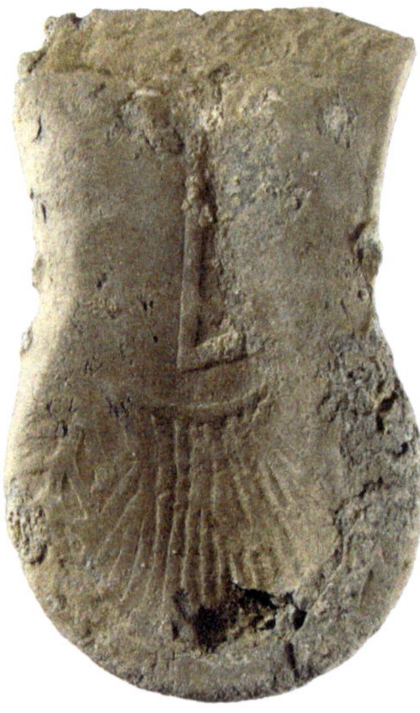

BUC-4DD52F, a
lead ampulla.

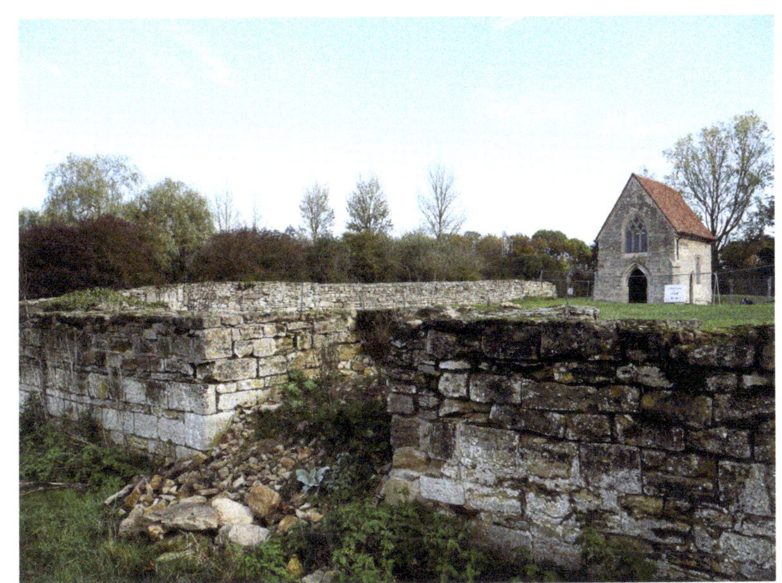

Bradwell Abbey.
(Arwen Wood
2019, courtesy of
the Milton Keynes
Discovery Centre)

BUC-76EA1F,
a copper alloy
mount of the
Virgin Mary
found in Lathbury,
dating to the
thirteenth century.

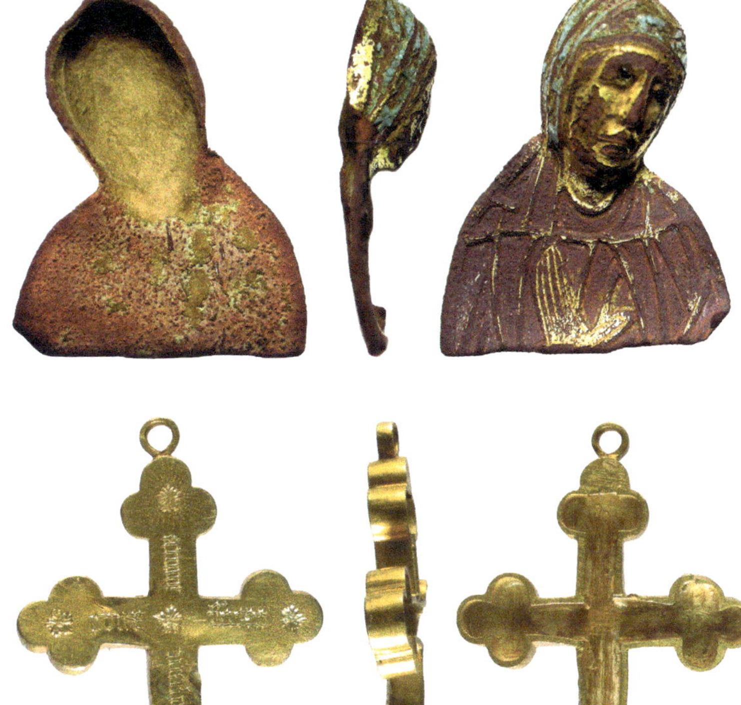

WMID-1006A0,
a possible gold
reliquary cross
dating to the
fifteenth century
AD, found
in Chicheley.

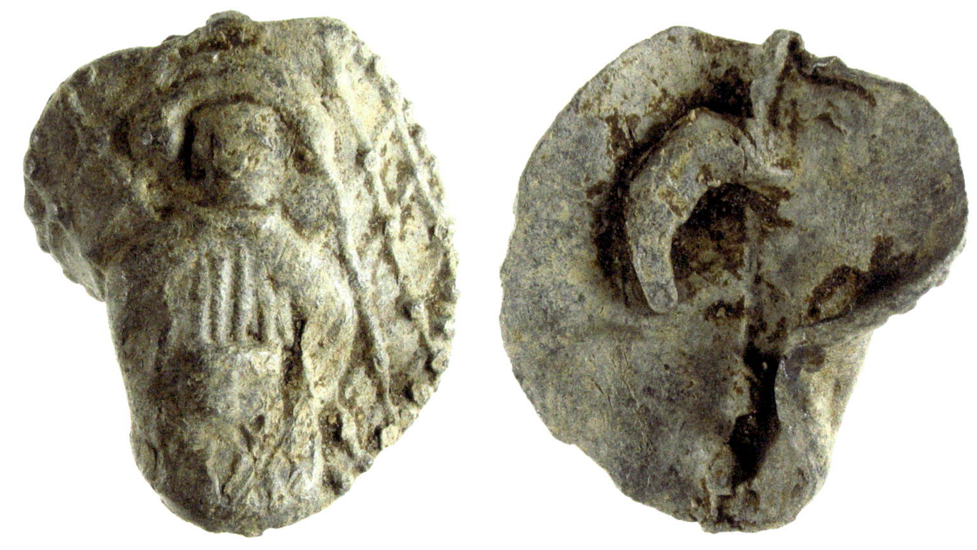

BUC-DE6120, a lead pilgrim badge dating to AD 1475–1530, found in Thornton.

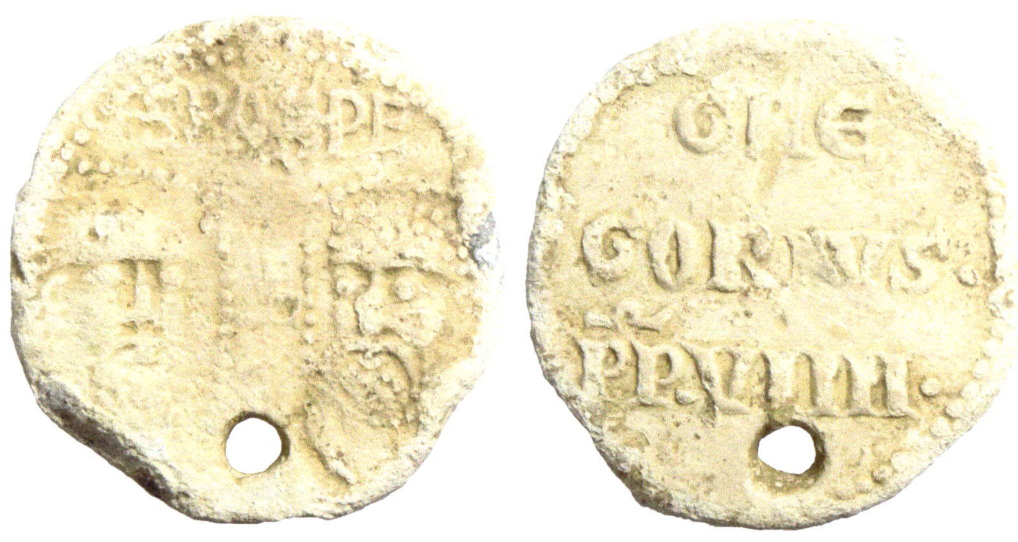

BUC-CB15D4, a lead papal bulla of Pope Gregory IX dating to AD 1227–41, found in Buckingham.

As seen in the previous chapter, stirrups first came into use in the early medieval period, having been unknown before that. The medieval period, however, saw the introduction of cast one-piece stirrups such as this one, with the suspension loop, side bars and footrest all part of the same object. Stirrups such as this more closely resemble the type that is in use today. The use of horses developed in this period, as up to the Norman invasion cavalry had played no part in war since the end of the Roman period. The mounted knight became the core around which armies and societies were built and was a high-status role in medieval life. It was further enshrined in myth and popular culture with the development of the cult of chivalry under Edward III. Chivalric romances, such as the stories of King Arthur and his knights, have had an enduring legacy on the culture of Western Europe.

The nobility from the thirteenth century onwards began to differentiate themselves and their retainers by wearing horse harness pendants decorated with heraldic designs. While, for much of the period, there was no real control over the designs, they were eventually codified, and the College of Arms still maintains records of these more official designs. The battlefield role of the mounted knight died out with the development of gunpowder weapons, which allowed even the lowliest person to kill the wealthiest, in spite of his armour. However, the ceremonial importance and status of the title can still be seen today with the honour of the title being handed out by the Queen.

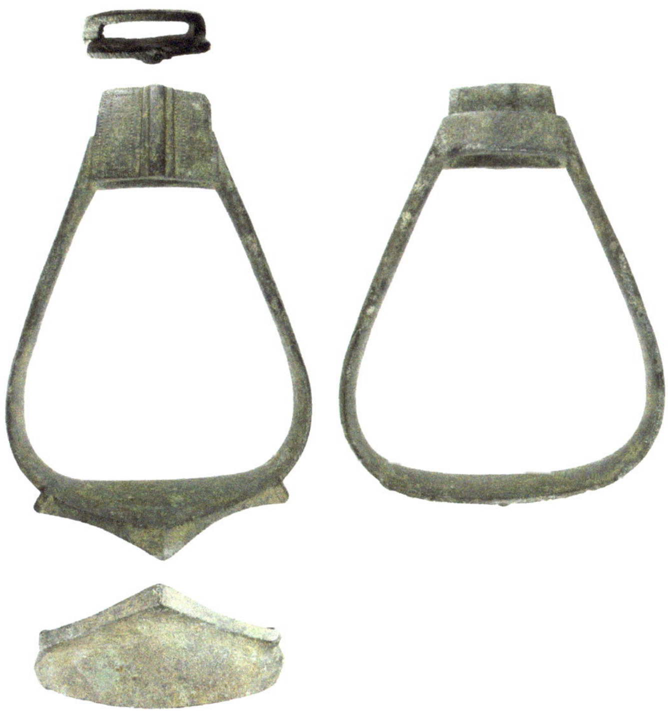

BUC-5D596F, a copper alloy stirrup.

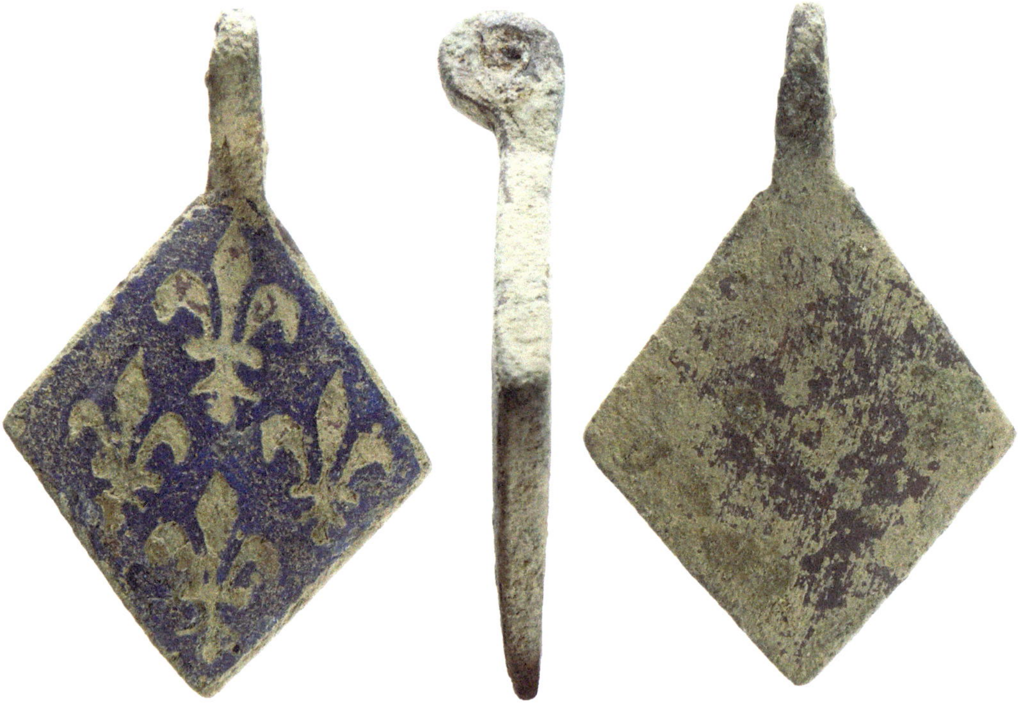

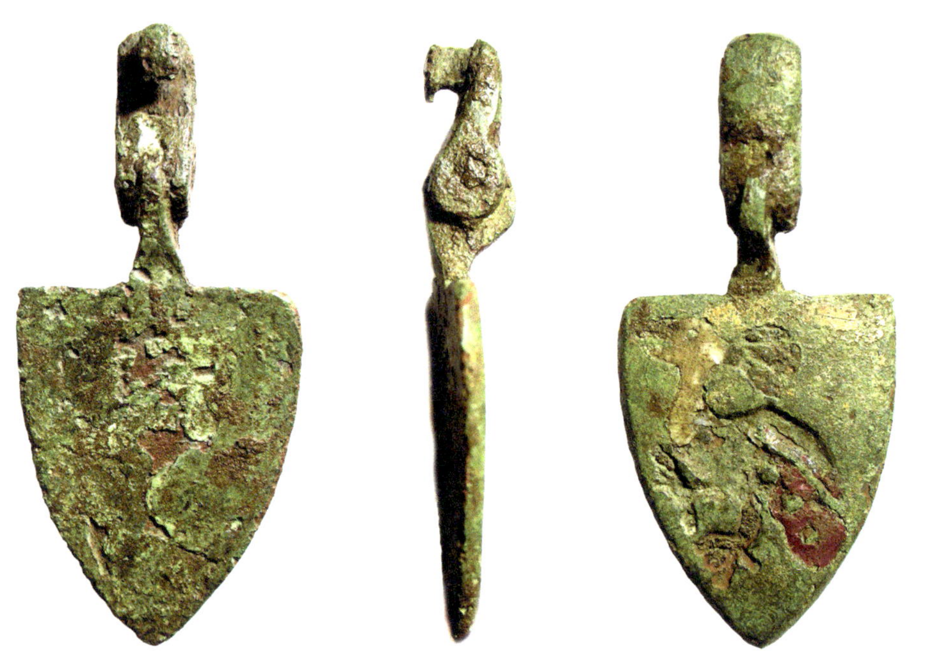

BUC-5A6F0C, a horse harness pendant found in Castlethorpe.

BUC-D8F293, a horse harness pendant found in Beachampton.

As Europe became more stable and centralised states developed, trade increased and was encouraged by monarchs and nobles who realised there was money to be made. There was a substantial increase in coinage, both English and foreign in use, and a monetarised economy last seen under Rome returned. England's main export for much of this period was cloth and textiles made from wool.

This object is a medieval folding balance, which would have been used as scales to weigh objects such as coins, jewellery, spices and medicines. A bowl would have hung at either end of the arms to contain the goods to be weighed. Goods would have been exchanged from across Europe, the Mediterranean and Scandinavia and foreign merchants would have been familiar sites in the ports and major cities. Conflicts, such as the Crusades, opened up new trade routes by providing access to the Silk Road, and goods such as spices and silk would have been accessible but an expensive commodity.

At a local level there was an increase in the sovereign awarding charters for markets, as this raised money for the crown. Monasteries also took advantage of this as the markets were encouraged to take place on monastic land. The scales would also have been used in this process for taxation and would have weighed foreign coins to check their weight against local currency.

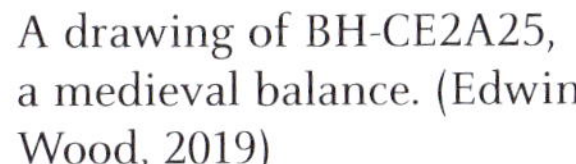

A drawing of BH-CE2A25, a medieval balance. (Edwin Wood, 2019)

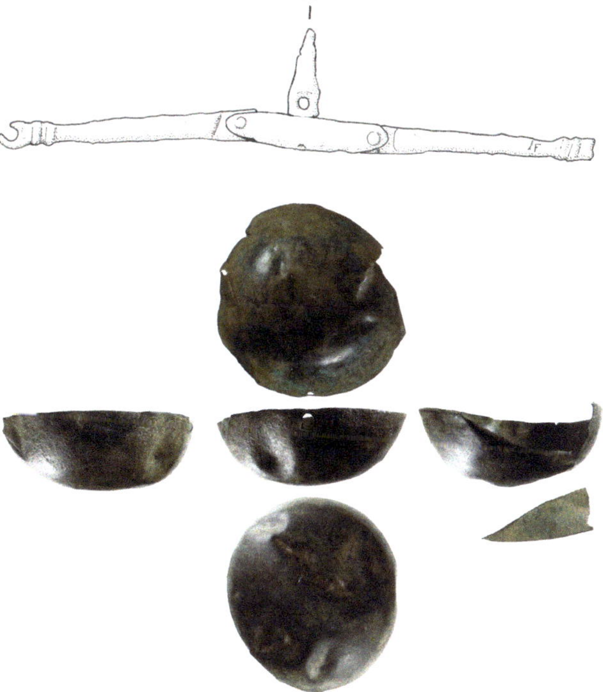

BUC-D8E07A, a scale pan found in Great Missenden.

This is the lower half of a silver needle case, a tube in which sewing needles would have been held. The case dates between AD 1150 and 1450 and was reported as treasure. Needle cases would have been worn on a belt or chain and were often grouped with other tools and implements such as keys and cosmetic tools. They were seen as a sign of social status as well as being useful, as needlecraft was a valued skill.

Needlework was strongly associated with women and the most famous work is the Bayeux Tapestry, which was sewn by the women of Canterbury. Due to the wool production women also would have been involved in spinning, and spindle whorls are often found dating to this period. However, men would also have been skilled in needlework, with tailors, soldiers, leather workers and many others carrying needle and thread as both a tool of their profession, or to make repairs while travelling.

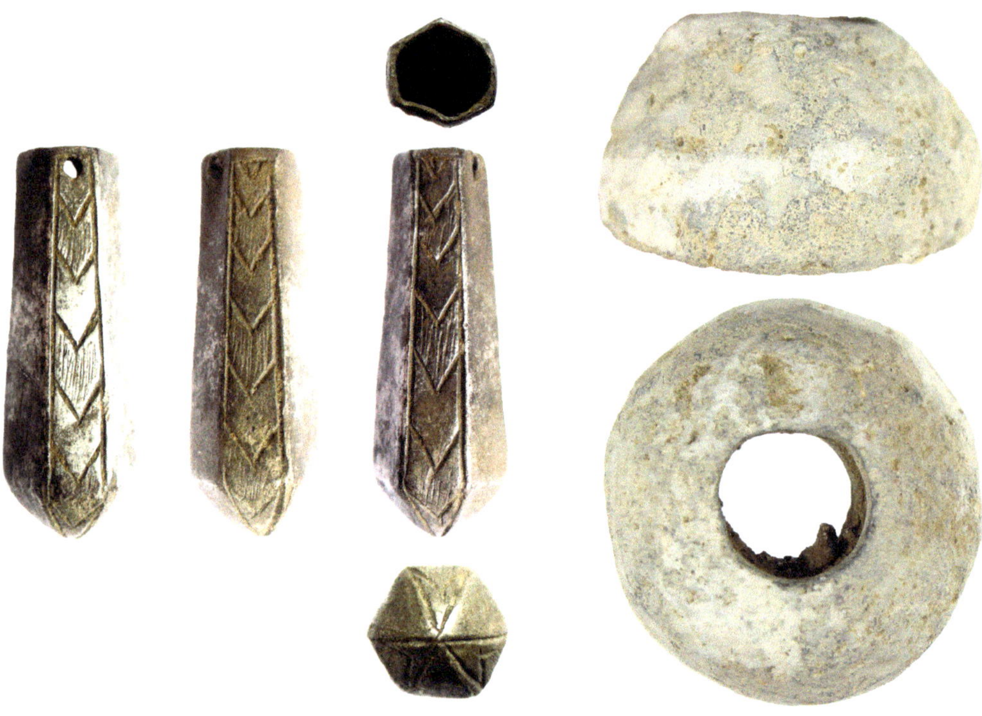

Above left: BUC-E30875, a needle holder.

Above right: BUC-31E7D7, a lead spindle whorl found in Thornton.

The medieval period saw England become an increasingly monetarised society, building on the work that had been done at the end of the early medieval period in the reigns of rulers such as Cnut and Edward the Confessor. Coins became more standardised, and there was an expansion of denominations in order to facilitate smaller everyday transactions and inflation. The cut halfpenny, literally a coin cut in half, was eventually replaced by a specifically designed round coin of the same value. England also maintained a relatively consistent silver standard for coins, something that is not seen in neighbouring countries, meaning that English coins were seen as more valuable. The same designs and legends were often used on coins by multiple rulers, especially pennies, making it very difficult to date and identify the ruler. This coin is a penny of Edward I dating to AD 1289–1291 and minted in London.

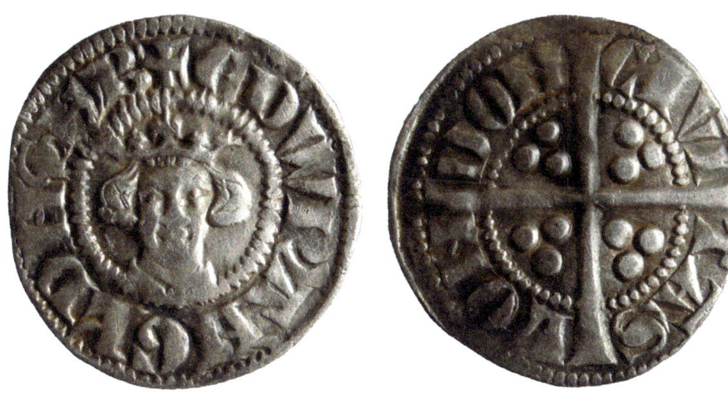

BUC-EEE9C6, a silver penny of Edward I.

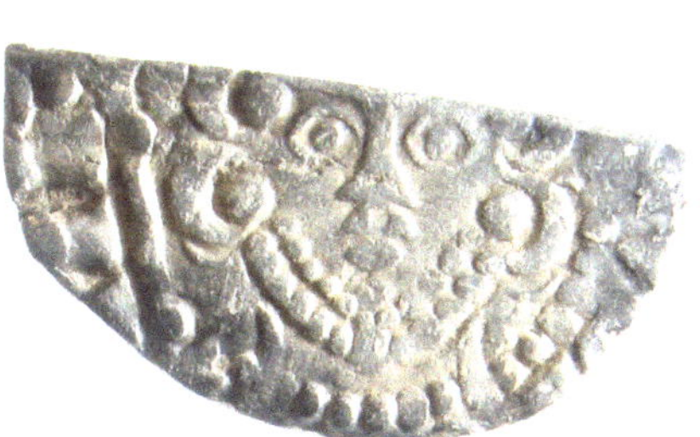

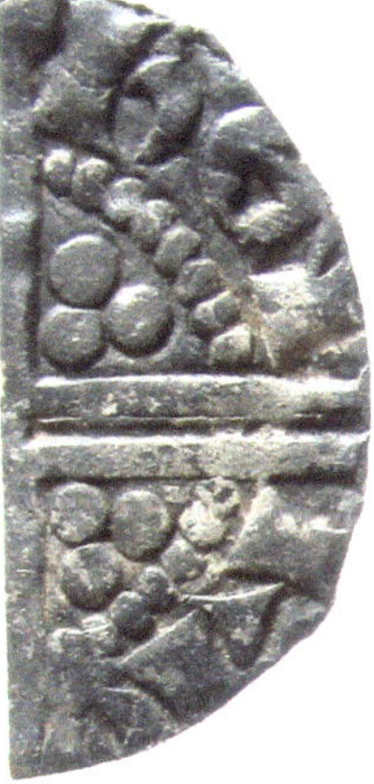

BUC-D1FC38, a halfpenny of Henry III dating to AD 1251–1272, found in Quainton.

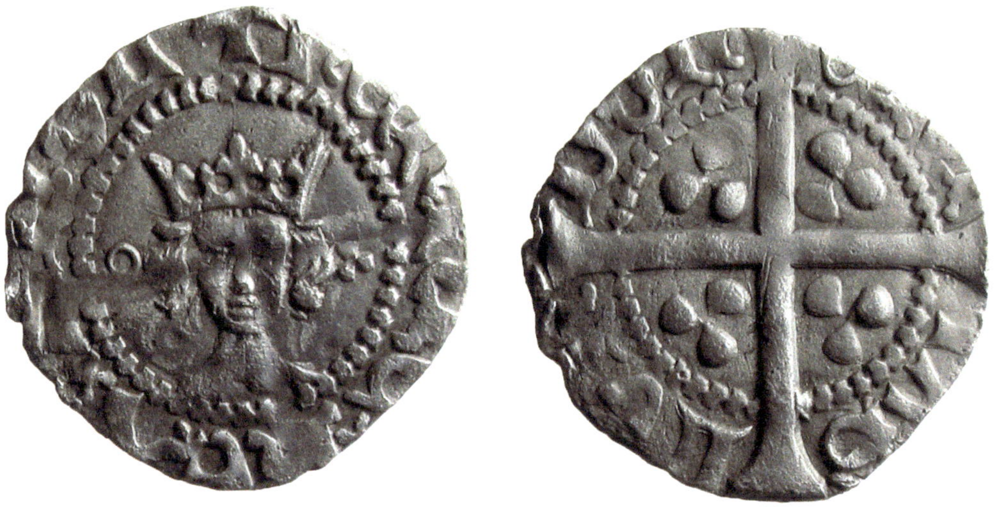

BUC-FE4A02, a silver halfpenny of Henry V dating to AD 1413–1422, found in Lacey Green

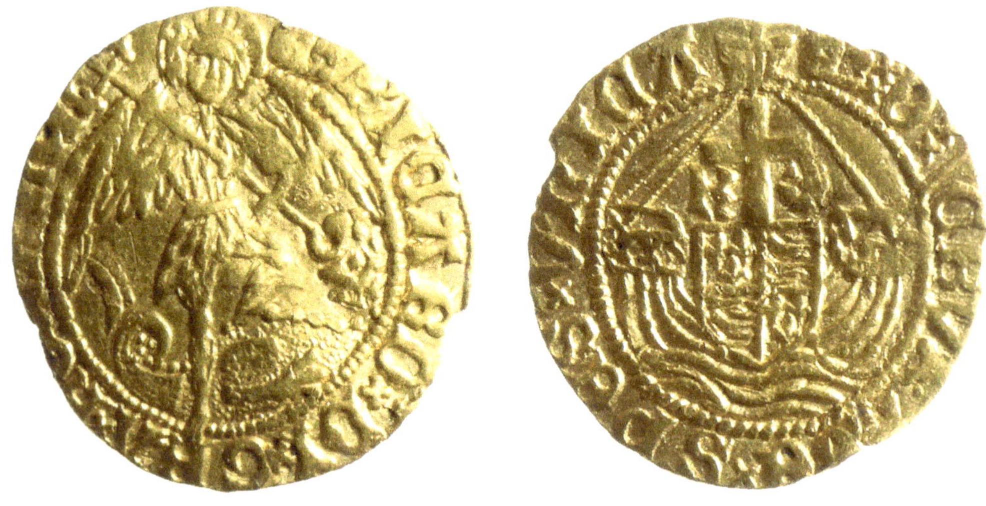

BUC-F502B8, a gold half angel of Richard III dating to AD 1483–1485, found in Buckingham.

This object is a complete copper alloy purse bar dating to *c*. AD 1450–1500. The purse bar consists of two sub-circular hoops that fold over each other. Running around the inside of each hoop are regular circular perforations, which would have originally attached to the fabric purse. It is unusual to find a complete purse bar like this, and usually only small parts of the purse bar remain.

The fabric purse or pouch was often made of leather or cloth and this part of the purse doesn't usually survive. However, traces are sometimes found on the objects that were contained within the pouch. Purses would have been worn by men and women and were used to carry coins and valuable belongings such as jewellery. Not all purses had a metal purse bar, and some were a simple drawstring pouch. The purses would have been worn on a belt hung round the waist, the idea being to openly display one's wealth by the size and weight of the purse. Such advertising, however, comes with a risk and thieves called 'cutpurses' would use knives to cut the fabric either completely away or enough to allow the contents to be stolen. Purses came in different styles and shapes as shown in the images here. Purse bars date from the late medieval period and are used into the early post-medieval period.

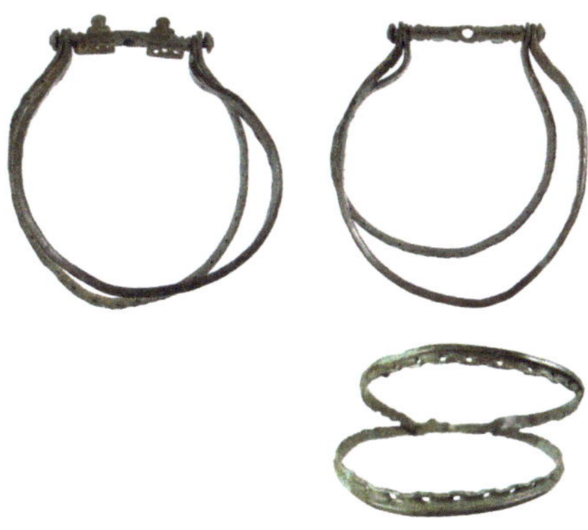

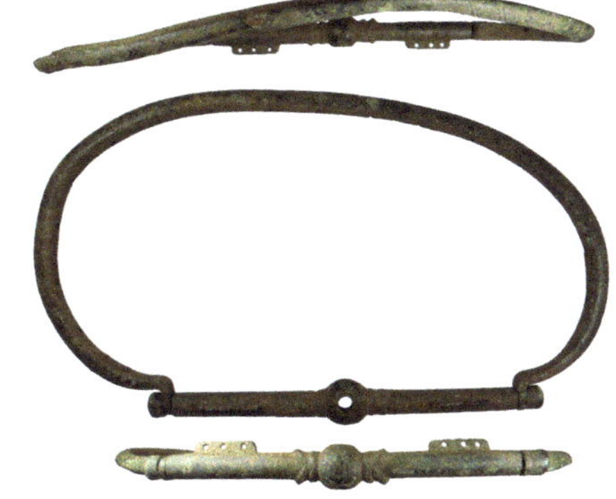

Above left: BUC-BEC031, a copper alloy purse bar.

Avove right: BUC-1485F2, a medieval to post-medieval purse bar dating to AD 1475–1575.

Right: BUC-25939D, a copper alloy purse bar dating from AD 1450–1500.

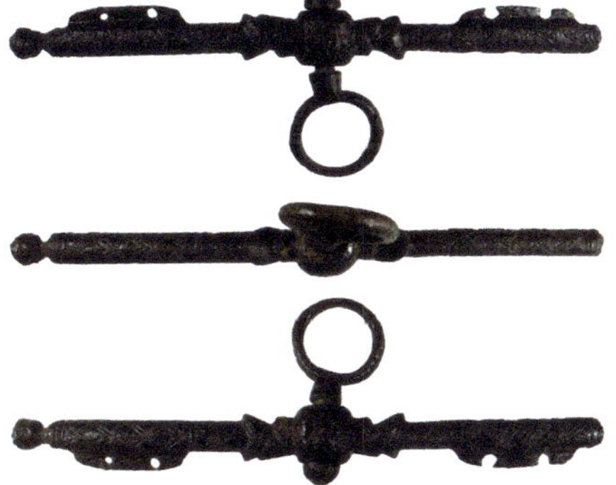

This is an iron arrowhead with a wide circular socket and barbed head. As the arrowhead is barbed it is likely it was used for hunting; its design is exactly the same as the barbed and tanged arrowhead discussed previously from the Late Neolithic–Early Bronze Age. Hunting was a popular pastime and an essential food source, providing meat to supplement the predominantly vegetarian diet of most people. Within the royal forests, permission was required in order to hunt, and in Buckinghamshire there were three royal forests and over fifty-six deer parks. Buckinghamshire's proximity to the City of London and Westminster made it the ideal leisure hunting area. Fishing also took place on rivers, and was monitored by various laws, including those set down by Magna Carta which controlled the use of fish traps.

Archery was a valuable military skill and, at various points during the medieval period, laws were introduced to ensure all men and boys were trained as archers to support the military campaigns. The heyday of the archer is often held to be the Hundred Years War, where the use of longbows contributed to the victories at the battles of Crécy, Poitiers and most famously Agincourt. A large number of bows were found preserved in the wreck of the *Mary Rose* and are now displayed alongside the ship in Portsmouth.

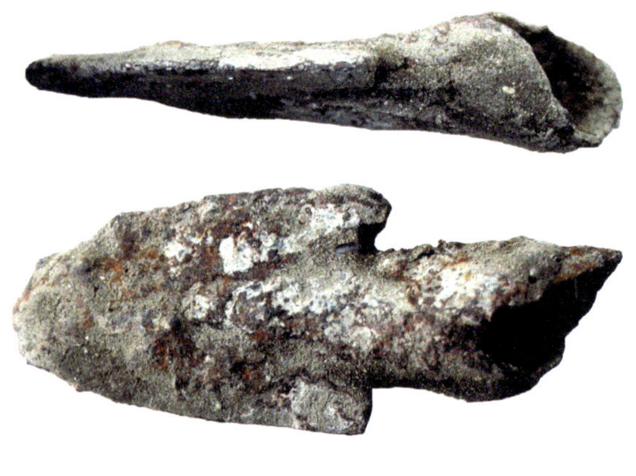

BUC-15CAB4, an iron arrowhead.

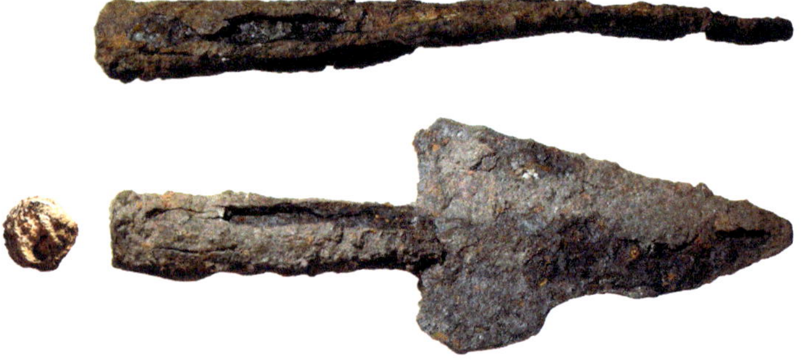

BUC-46E4F2, an iron arrowhead found in Weston Turville.

Items of jewellery were often given as tokens of love or friendship; posy rings are the most famous examples, with inscriptions inside their bands. However, other objects also carry such designs, such as this an annular brooch, with the inscription 'AMIE AMEI' running around the outside of the frame. The inscription translates as '[to a] loyal friend' and is a touching reminder of the personal relationships that are too often hidden or forgotten in the study of the past. The brooch is only 1.1 cm in diameter, suggesting that the brooch was used for decoration and would not have fastened clothing. Its size suggests that it was also designed to be viewed close up, meaning that anyone reading the inscription would have been within the owner's intimate personal space. Brooches were worn by both men and women, and like today they were used to show individual taste or sometimes allegiance to a religious, political or important social group such as a guild.

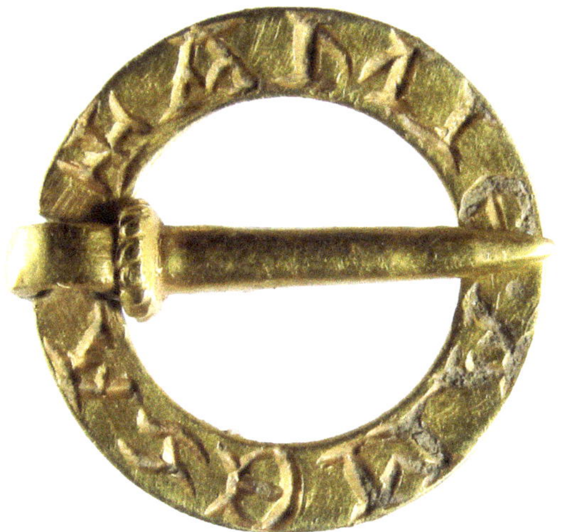 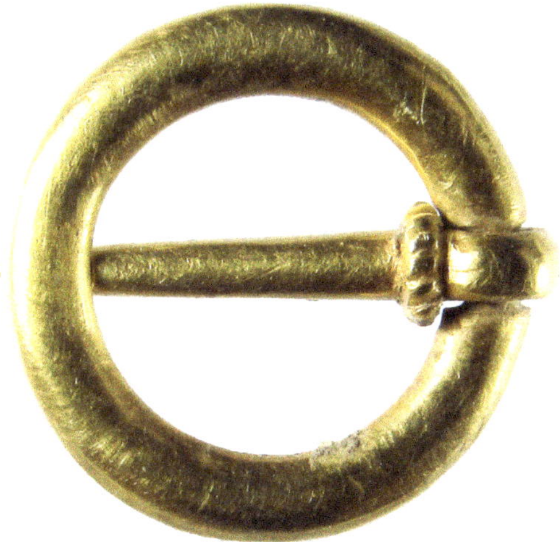

BUC-B93E93, a gold annular brooch.

Chapter 7
Post-medieval to Modern Period

In AD 1485, the Battle of Bosworth saw Henry VII take the throne and found the Tudor dynasty. The medieval period began its slow transition into the post-medieval and then Early Modern period so that by the death of the last Tudor, Elizabeth I in AD 1603, England had left the medieval world far behind. This is a period of great change, where the remnants of medieval society were swept away, and it encompasses some of our most famous historical figures and events such as Henry VIII and the Civil War. The religion of the nation would be changed, and the power of the monarch curbed, before the accession of Hanoverians at the start of the eighteenth century brought the period to a close.

The Civil War took place between AD 1642 and 1651 and affected Buckinghamshire greatly. Nearby Oxford became the centre for the Royalist court, with London the centre for Parliament. This put Buckinghamshire in between the two territories, with the roads through the county linking the two centres. While none of the large battles took place within the county, smaller skirmishes happened at Wendover, High Wycombe and Chalgrove field, where John Hampden was fatally wounded. Hampden was a leading MP and Parliamentarian, an opponent of the unchecked power of the crown. In 1642 he was one of the five members of Parliament that King Charles I attempted, unsuccessfully, to arrest in the House of Commons, thus precipitating the Civil War. His statue stands today in the Market Square, Aylesbury, and at the entrance to the Palace of Westminster.

The Industrial Revolution saw transportation and industry change across the county, with the development of the canal system in the eighteenth century providing links between London and the country. This meant goods and people could be moved across long distances, connecting the cities and towns with the coalfields and raw materials of the North and Midlands. The canal network through Buckinghamshire connected London to Northamptonshire, with separate arms linking Aylesbury, Wendover and Buckingham. The arrival of the railways in the nineteenth century meant that instead of Aylesbury being a full day's travel from London, it could be reached in hours by goods and people.

As in previous periods metal artefacts are the most commonly recorded. Throughout the period there was an increase in the use of copper alloy and cast-iron cooking equipment, with the latter becoming more widely available as the Industrial Revolution progressed.

Ceramics, such as locally produced Brill ware or imported items such as Bellarmine (or Bartmann) jugs, formed the most common tableware.

In the last century two world wars and the expansion of London's hinterland and commuter belt have done more to alter the landscape of the county. Technology has advanced at a pace unseen at any point in history, from the computer-sized computers built at Bletchley Park to crack the enigma code to the modern smart phone. The manors and country houses of the elite took on new roles, as at Disreali's Hughenden Manor – a secret centre for map making in the Second World War. The landscape of the county may yet be altered still as major infrastructure works like HS2 look set to bring change on a scale not seen for generations.

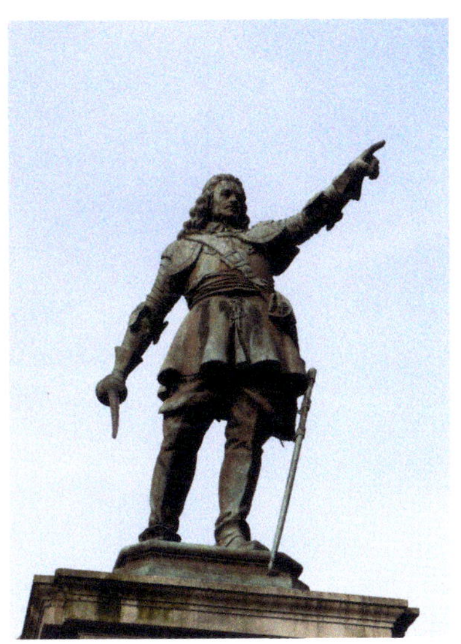

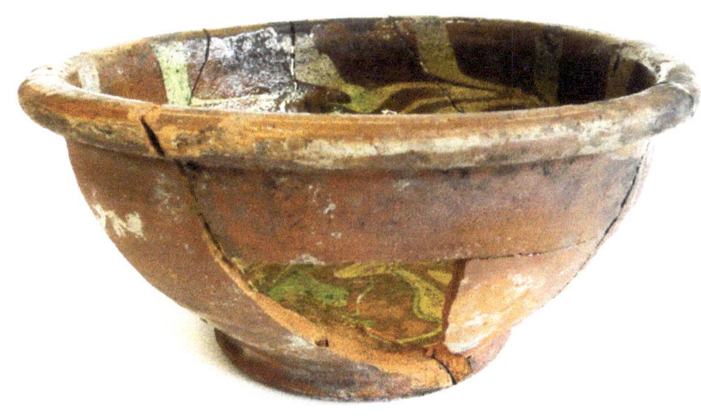

Above left: Statue of John Hampden in Aylesbury. (Arwen Wood, 2019)

Above right: A Brillware bowl dating from eighteenth century found in Cuddington, AYBCM 32.77. (Arwen Wood/BCM, 2019)

Right: Bellarmine (or Bartmann) jug found in Winslow. (Arwen Wood/BCM, 2019)

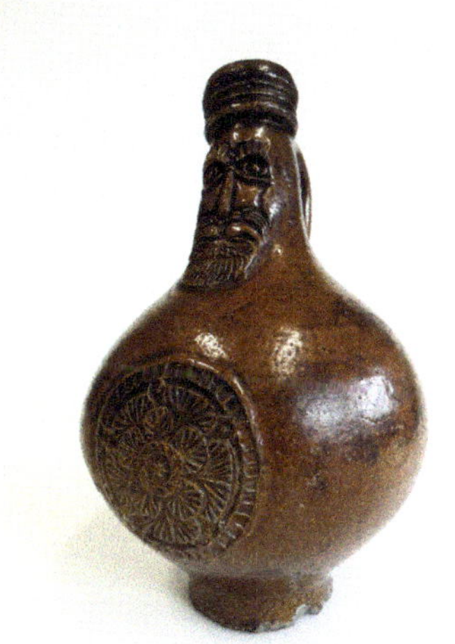

Falconry, or hunting with birds, had been a popular pasttime since the medieval period and continued to be so into the seventeenth century. This vervel or hawking ring was attached to the bird and was designed to show that the bird was owned rather than wild. The types of birds that were used for hunting were predominantly falcons, such as peregrines and kestrels. It was expensive to train the bird, so it was a hobby for the wealthy part of society. Vervels were fastened to the bird either on its leg, or on a strap attached to the bird and carried the owner's name and address. This is unusual for a historical object to give the name and location of the owner, and really gives an insight into the past that is not usually available.

This vervel is inscribed with the name 'Robert Erle Carmarvin' or Robert Dormer (1610–1643), the first Earl of Carnarvon. The shield has the crest of Robert Dormer, who became the Lord Lieutenant of Buckinghamshire in 1641. Charles I had been guardian to Robert Dormer and he was, for a while, the keeper of the king's hawks. He was killed at the Battle of Newbury in 1643 during the Civil War and is buried at All Saint's Church in Wing, having originally been buried in the chapel of Jesus College, Oxford.

The use of birds in hunting declined through the seventeenth century and was replaced by shoots using guns. However, this would result in the meat potentially being spoilt by the lead shot, so other methods such as the use of duck decoys, an idea imported from the Netherlands, were also used. Buckinghamshire has one of the few remaining duck decoys in the country at Borstal, now a wildlife haven owned by the National Trust.

Vervels are not often found, and the ones that have been recorded have all been found by metal detectorists, showing how important it is to record objects to expand the archaeological record.

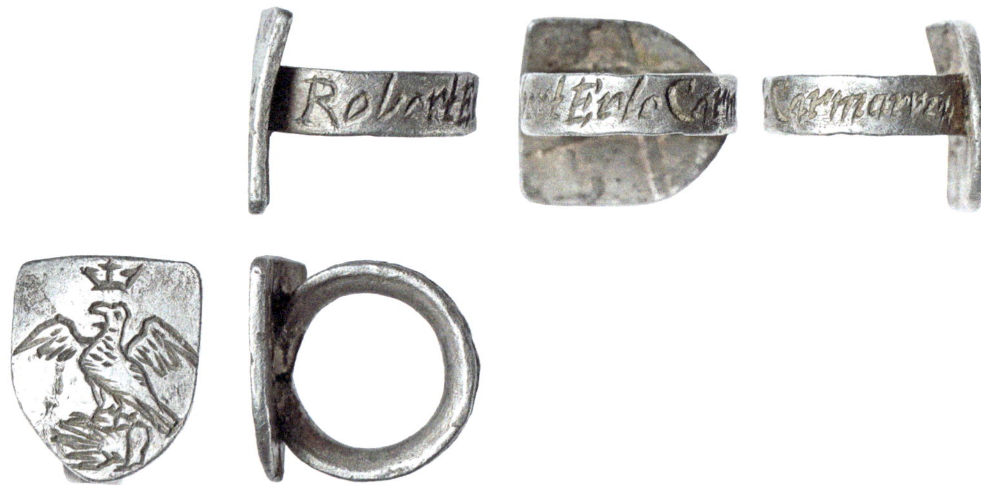

BH-D528FA, a silver vervel.

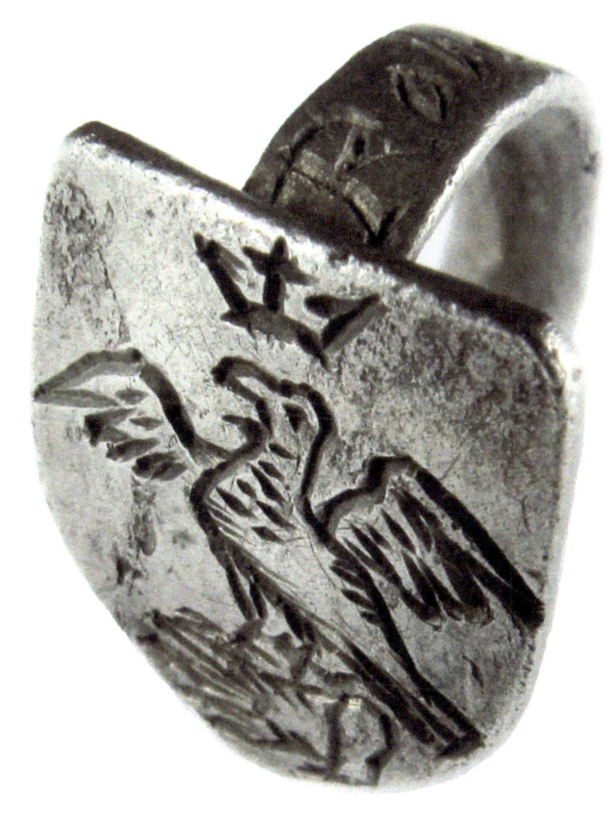

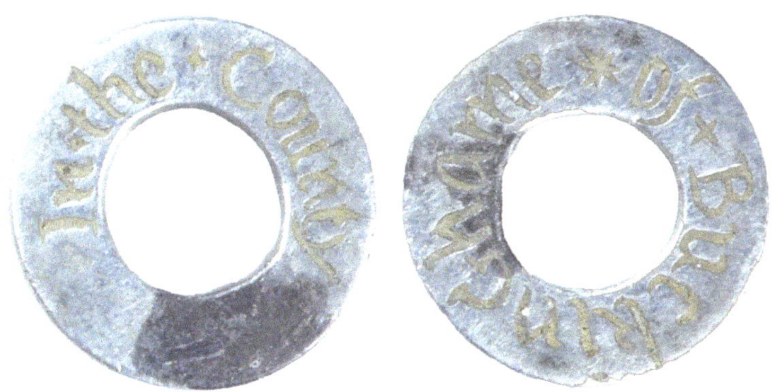

BUC-D9DCD5, a vervel found in Little Missenden, inscribed 'in the county of Buckinghame'.

This is a lead powder measure in the form of a small open cup with a sub-circular base, dating from the sixteenth to seventeenth century AD. This would have been the cap of the powder measure – a bottle-shaped object that would have held the charge for one musket shot. The lugs on the side of the cap would have attached it to the measure so that it wasn't lost. The powder bottles were worn across the chest of a soldier attached to a leather strap called a bandolier. Each belt would have held twelve powder bottles, which is why they're often known as apostles.

Powder measures such as this would have been used in the Civil War. Other objects that are found from this turbulent time include musket shot, buckles from spurs and belts, and sword fittings. Depictions of Charles I have also been found in the county, including this silver medal depicting the king and his wife, Henrietta Maria, probably belonging to a Royalist sympathiser. Such depictions became very popular after the restoration of the monarchy in 1660 as a way of showing allegiance to the new regime.

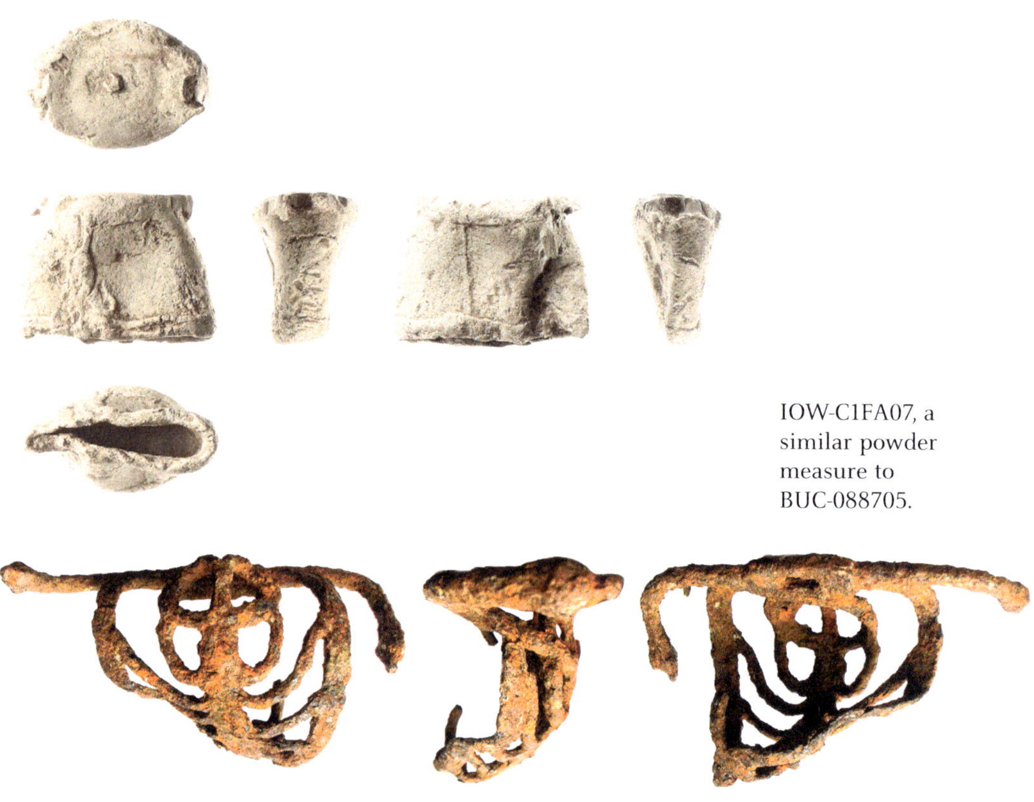

IOW-C1FA07, a similar powder measure to BUC-088705.

BUC-A3CCA7, an iron sword hilt dating from the seventeenth century, found in Quainton.

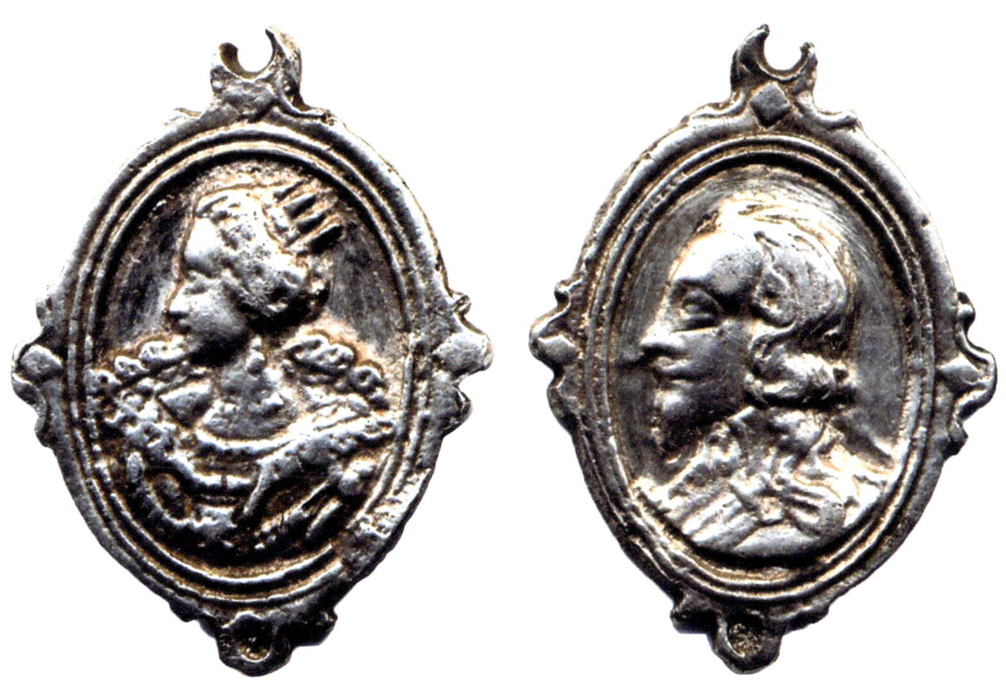

BUC-575178, a silver medal depicting Charles I and his wife, Henrietta Maria, found in Medmenham.

This gold finger ring is unusual, and no obvious parallels were found when it went through the treasure process in 2002. It dates from AD 1500–1700 and is cast with a figure of a fox lying down on the bezel. On the inside of the hoop the ring bares the inscription 'THE FOX IS BEST SERWD WHEN HE GOETH OF HIS ARND HIM SELFE'. It is a strange inscription, possibly referring to the recipient of the ring as the 'fox', or it may mean that a person is at their best when they achieve their own work. Rings with inscriptions are more common in the post-medieval period, with mourning rings and posy rings the most common forms of inscribed jewellery.

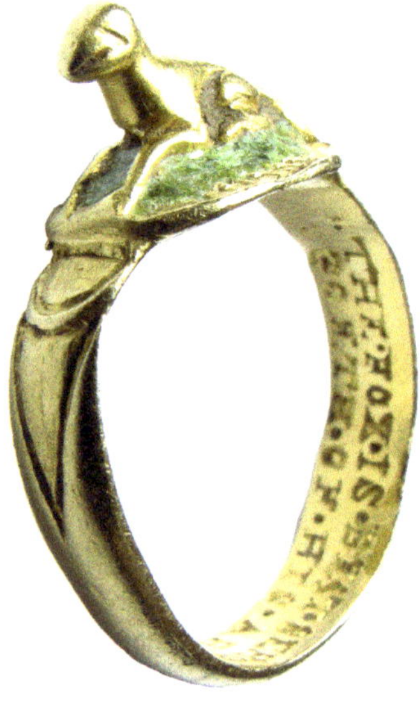

PAS-37DA54, a gold finger ring.

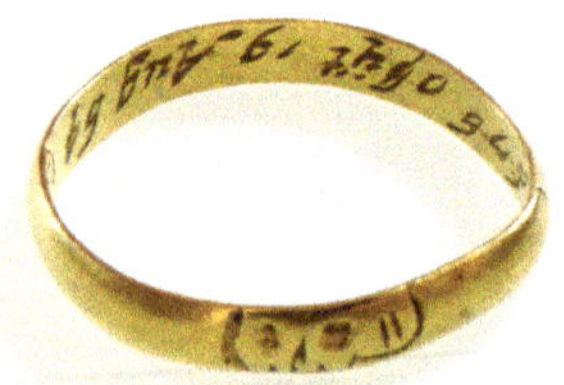

BUC-087696, a mourning ring found in Soulbury dating from *c.* 1600. The inscription reads 'S R Aged 76 obijt 19 Aug 64'.

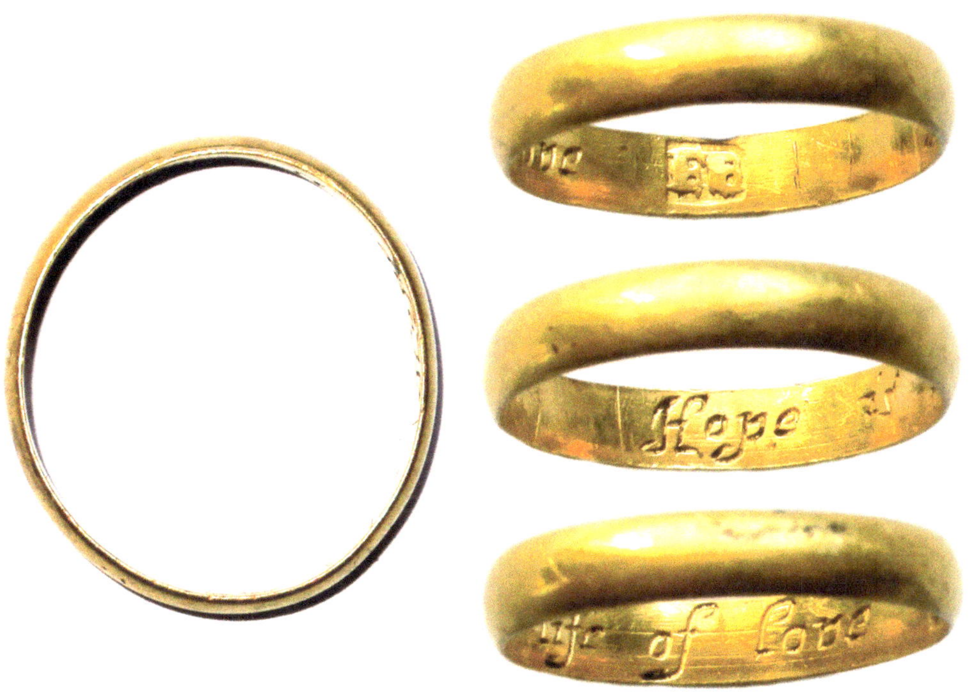

SUR-923A04, a gold posy ring found in Brill dating to *c.* 1700. Inscription reads 'Hope is the life of love'.

On the Portable Antiquities Scheme database, priority is given to record finds over 300 years old, with good findspot information. However, occasionally finds are brought in that are unique or of significance to the local area.

One such example is this medallion or medal of John Wilkes (1727–97) dating from AD 1768. John Wilkes was the MP for Aylesbury and Middlesex and also a journalist. He was also a member of the infamous Hellfire Club, a high society group that met at the West Wycombe Hellfire Caves. The Hellfire Club had many known members at this time and was infamous for its activities that were thought of as pagan and involved mock rituals usually involving a lot of drink, and activities of a sexual nature. Wilkes was outspoken and his campaigning for freedom of press by publishing risqué documents, criticising government and the king, resulted in him being expelled from Parliament. His activities also meant that he spent two years in gaol from 1768–70, which this medal commemorates. Known as an advocate of the people and for liberty, Wilkes supported the American rebels during the War of Independence, something that did little to endear him to the king and government. The obverse of the medallion depicts John Wilkes facing right, with the inscription 'John Wilkes Esq'. On the reverse is the figure of Time inscribing a pyramid with '45/BRITON/ MAGNA/CHARTA'. Below this is inscribed 'In memory of the year MDCCLXVIIV', or 1768. A similar medallion can be seen in the National Portrait Gallery.

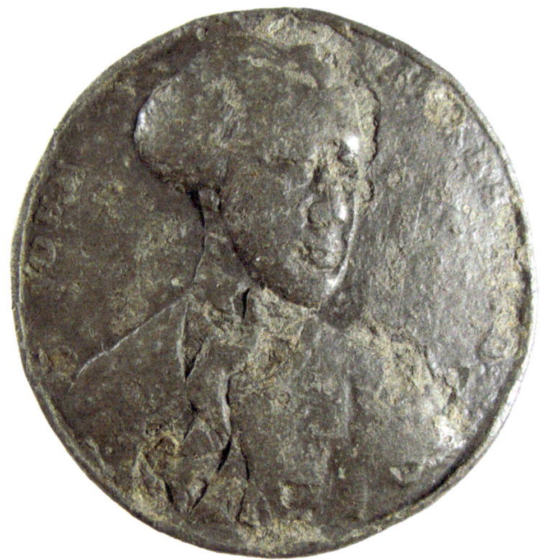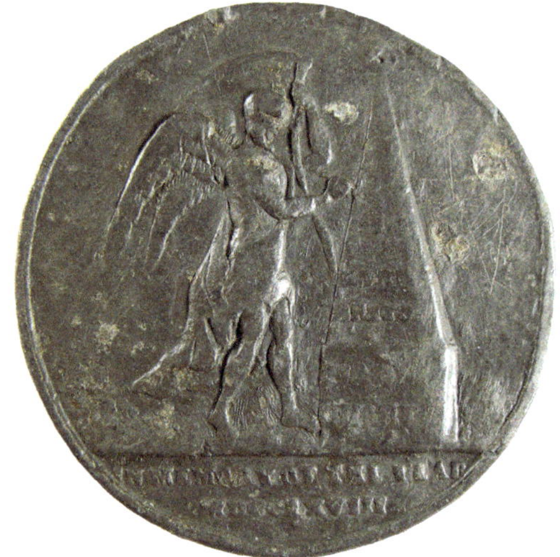

BUC-5E6B0A, a medallion of John Wilkes.

Occasionally finds are brought in for recording that are completely unexpected, and this one was one of these objects. This is a silver pocket watch dating to around AD 1694, and so falling just within the boundaries of the Treasure Act. The outside of the case is decorated to represent a scallop shell and opens to reveal the watch dial. The back plate is engraved with the Latin phrase 'Oswald Durant Fecit' or 'Oswald Durant made this'. Watches such as this are known as 'form' watches and became fashionable in the early seventeenth century. By knowing the maker of the watch, it is actually possible to date it quite precisely. Oswald Durant was involved in the formation of the Clockmakers Company, founded in 1631, and one of its first members. He became warden for the company in 1645, and only one other pocket watch is known to be made by him: a watch in the shape of a book.

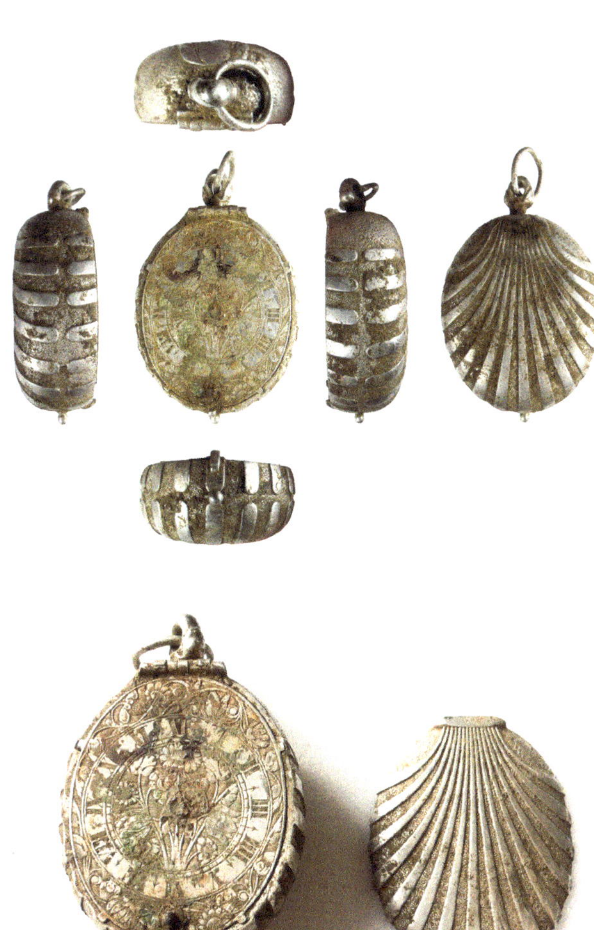

BUC-7A4E6C, a silver
pocket watch.

The post-medieval period saw the arrival of tobacco to Britain. Traditionally it was thought to have been brought back by Sir Walter Raleigh in 1586, but it is likely that tobacco was brought in earlier by Spanish and Portuguese traders. Tobacco smoking became a popular habit and finds relating to it are often discovered, with the most common being clay pipes.

Pipe tampers were used to pack down the tobacco into the bowl and were often elaborately decorated. This pipe tamper dates from AD 1700–1800 and the owner must have had a cheeky sense of humour given the subject matter. The tamper depicts a female figure who is holding up her skirt, apparently to urinate. The tamper is interesting for the insight it offers into what women would have worn at the time. This figure seems to have an elaborate hair style or bonnet, and details can be seen in the dress which are typical of the eighteenth century. Smoking paraphernalia often depicted crude and lewd scenes such as this and are generally associated with men.

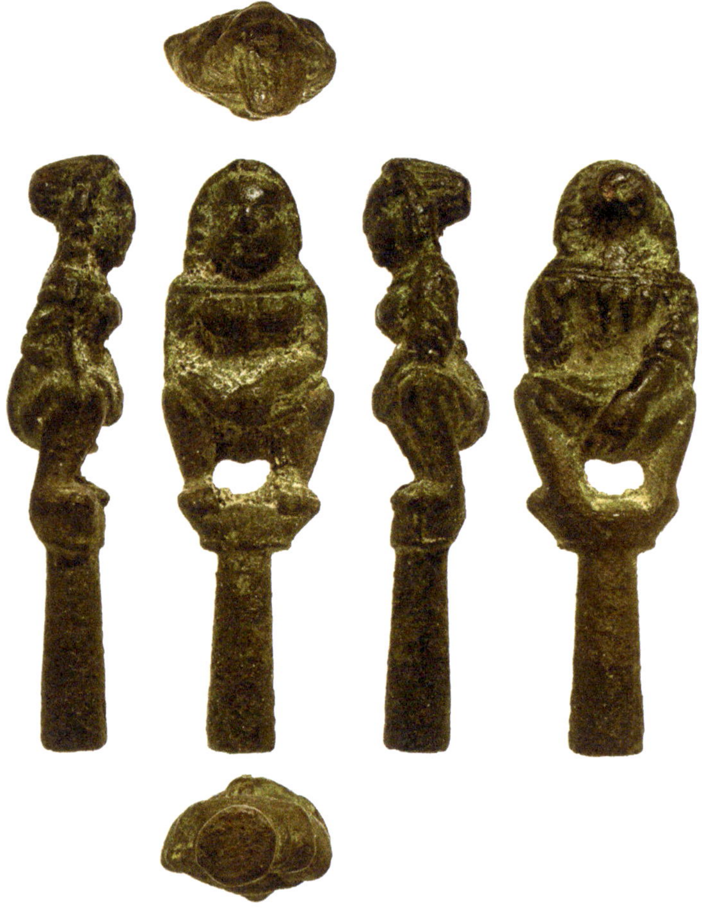

SWYOR-C3DE5C, a
pipe tamper.

Seal matrices are common finds and were used to make an impression into a wax. This would have authenticated a document, and also it could be used to seal it closed. Seal matrices come in a wide range of motifs, from merchant seals to crests of dignitaries, and give an insight into different social classes and the types of documents needed in everyday life. The design on this seal matrix has the shield and crest of Sir Philip Pauncefort-Duncombe, created baronet in 1859, who lived at Great Brickhill, Buckinghamshire. This seal matrix has a suspension loop at the top, so it was likely to have been attached to a chain or string that could be worn. Seal matrices are used from the early medieval to the modern period.

The distribution of finds can be a good indicator of how much contact there was across the world, both with trade and with travelling, and can often be surprising. This is a tobacco pipe dating from the late nineteenth to early twentieth century and is from the Mahsikulumbwe tribe in Zambia. The pipe itself is zoomorphic and depicts either an antelope or a buffalo. The bowl sits on the animal's back and only a small part of it remains. Pipes like this are rare finds in Britain and are thought to be tourist souvenirs brought back from the country. This object is a historical find and was found twenty years ago when workers were excavating a trench to lay some pipes. It has now been donated by the finder to the Old Gaol Museum in Buckingham.

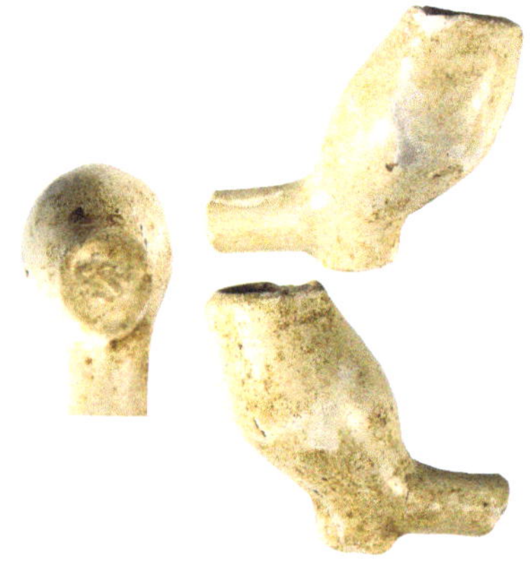

BERK-800D25, a clay pipe found in Kingsey dating to the seventeenth century AD.

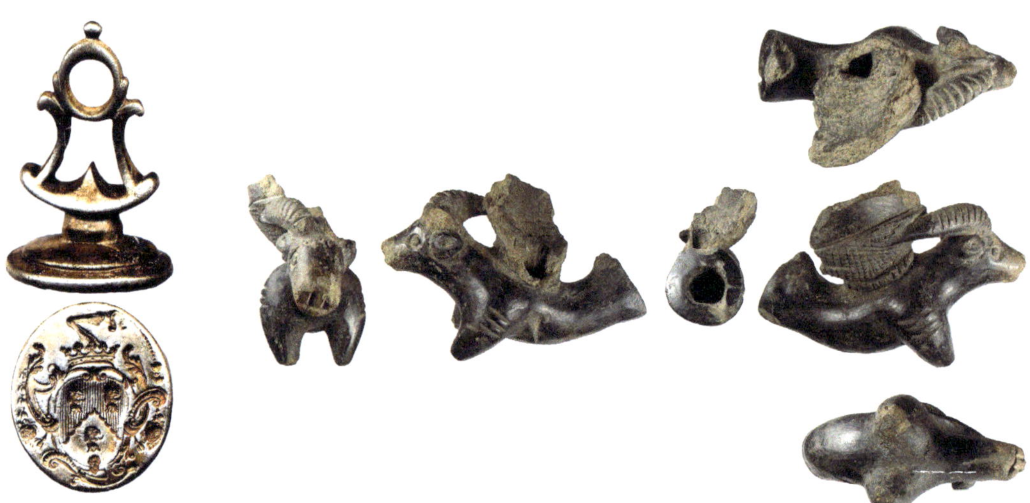

Above left: BUC-6B6BC7, a silver seal matrix.

Above right: BUC-282AE0, a ceramic tobacco pipe.